PERMISSION TO BE TOUGH!

RAISING BOYS TO BE RUGGED GENTLEMEN

ADVANCE PRAISES

RAISING RUGGED GENTLEMEN was always a goal of my dad's when it came to me and my brother. The essence of a rugged gentleman, as I understand it from the years of growing up with my dad, is being prepared for whatever life throws your way. Whether that is a formal event where manners and etiquette are required, or a self-defense scenario where strength and courage could be the difference between life and death. However, just being prepared isn't enough to be a rugged gentleman, an ability to discern the appropriate reaction to the given situation is also crucial.

My dad made sure his sons have a working knowledge of a variety of subjects: from etiquette to craftsmanship; from woodsmanship to sportsmanship and respect are just a few traits of the rugged gentleman. Over time I have learned that the true rugged gentleman takes responsibility for his destiny. He knows that if he wants security, he must be formidable, if he wants respect, he must be courageous and have morals, and if he wants fulfillment then he must put others before himself. These are the lessons given to me by my father, and the lessons I will work hard to impart on my son.

~ William Austin

GOD BLESSED ME with both a girl and a boy child, and I applaud the author for the awareness that the world does, indeed, need "gentlemen" but that they need not lose their masculine strength in character in the process. We are surrounded today with elements of the #MeToo movement, where references are made about respect for women and setting boundaries for social, professional, and myriad aspects of dating. It is our job as parents to question what we do to raise children who respect others.

We are responsible to instill in our sons the aspects of being rugged enough to stand for their principles yet understand how a gentleman shows respect for others...to exercise intentional actions in consistent, practical ways as promoted in a book I believe is timeless.

~T R Stearns
Retired Superintendent of Schools

IT MIGHT SEEM impossible to recognize a gentleman when you see him! In front of you may stand a Pierce Brosnan type in a flashy dinner jacket, or someone in jeans and a beard. Rich men in expensive suits may have never gotten the memo about growing up...

Over the years, I've watched my sons become good men—men who exhibit kindness, respect for women, appreciation for the love and support of their choice of life mates, and love and open affection for their children. I see a healthy dose of being open, warm, vulnerable, and humane.

Rugged Gentlemen is a reminder of what life will be for boys who grow up starved for the touch and guidance of a role model who can teach them more than being an aggressive hunter in control of life. They may never find the joy in honoring the humanity in everyone or being quick to share a smile. It is most likely they will lack basic manners, fear being open and friendly, or fencing others off with sex, race, creed, or religion.

This book offers a deeper understanding...and many options to step up and make a difference. Austin has a deep awareness of the impact of "growing" boys...to show them how to navigate the world as gentlemen; he is clear there is no better person to take on this role model than a loving father—or when necessary, a strong and loving mother.

Today, it is clear there is an urgency to tackle the issues addressed by the author...the adorable baby boys we see create an excitement of a new generation of males, and how we can be responsible to raise good brothers, sons and fathers. We have the opportunity to raise more gentlemen... even if they are more comfortable in their jeans than expensive suits.

~ Anna Weber, Literary Strategist
Voices in Print

———————

I have to "weigh-in" by asking and answering the question, "What's it like to be raised by and being around Rugged Gentlemen?" You see, as the daughter of this author, my life has been sculpted in myriad ways—all by the way my father "chose" to raise his sons! He established my beliefs and expectations.

Have you ever walked alone down a street at night, and gotten a creepy feeling that someone or something is following or watching you, and felt vulnerable and a little bit helpless? In the moment what I would typically think about—besides how I could defend myself—is how nice it would be to have someone by my side to protect me. The first figure or man that pops into your mind when you think of who you wish could be there with you is probably a rugged gentleman.

If I had to come up with a checklist for women, borne of understanding my father's parenting style, to determine if a significant other, crush, or friend is a rugged gentleman it would look something like this:

Do you feel safe when you are around him?

Do you feel as though he would step up to protect you from harm, and are you also positive he would never cause any harm to you?

Is he able to express and control his emotions?

Do you feel confusion about his feelings for you or has he provided clarity and leadership throughout the entirety of your relationship? When he is frustrated, does he express it with words and seek reconciliation or is he passive aggressive, leaving you wondering if you are the reason behind his frustrations?

Does he stand firm in his morals and decisions?

This question isn't quite as black and white as others. A rugged gentleman will not allow the opinions of man to constitute his morals, he will do what he believes is right even under scrutiny and stress. However, he will also have the humility to admit when he has made a mistake or a bad decision. A man who leads well in a marriage will have the strength to make decisions and stick to them and he will also have the strength to own up to his mistakes.

Does he treat others with respect whether they are strangers or not?

Does he talk to his mother in a respectful manner? If he doesn't then maybe consider how he's going to treat you when you're the mother of his children. Does he also speak to waiters and store clerks in a respectful manner? Observing the manner in which he treats people with whom he may never come in contact with again says a lot about his value for humanity.

Does he celebrate with you in the good times and mourn with you in the bad?

Galatians 6 is relevant to fulfilling the law of Christ—to bear the burdens of each other. If God is commanding these men to bear one another's burdens, then surely that must be his command for the modern-day rugged gentleman as well. Does the man you have in mind view caring for others as a privilege or is it more of a chore that should really be left for the women to carry out?

Obviously, this checklist is not exclusive, there are many other factors, which go into being a rugged gentleman...I will leave them for you to read in my father's words! These are the main aspects that come to mind when I think about the idea of a rugged gentleman and the ways in which I was raised.

Being around my dad and brothers brings me a sense of safety. I know that if a situation arises their first instinct will be to protect me, and I am also sure that they would never purposefully put me in harm's way.

When I was disciplined as a child, the punishment and reasons behind the punishment were delivered in a loving way, which at the time may have felt painful but no longer cause discomfort. I remember the situations because they truly were what was best for me.

I would say my dad was always willing to make the hard decisions when it came to what was best for the family. I saw him take risks with starting businesses and moving us to the other side of Colorado which I know were not the easiest decisions to make. He kept our well-being in mind and stuck to his decisions even when I complained the three longs months up to—and months after—we moved. He deeply understood being a rugged gentleman—and lives accordingly.

I've been taught the importance of respect from my parents. I've seen my dad model it when I watched him interact with me and my friends as well as the people we still encounter when we go out to eat or go shopping.

My dad has always been the first one to celebrate my accomplishments with me, and he's been there in the hard times too. My emotions are not below him.

If you read this, as a young woman, I hope this checklist is helpful when assessing a future husband—or if you read it as a young man, analyzing yourself to see if you truly are a rugged gentleman—know these things are not ultimatums. We are human, and actions are not going to be carried out perfectly by any man on Earth. The bigger goal is to be aware.

Writing about this was hard. My father established such expectations, I found myself drifting to the flaws I may have seen in the men around me. If my checklist were the ultimate determinant, most probably wouldn't be considered rugged gentlemen. My dad taught me, however, to ask a bigger question, "is this the type of man he IS STRIVING TO BE? You might experience a degree of uncontrolled anger or some insensitivity, but when you consider the big picture and his overall demeanor does he make you proud to be associated with him—or do you feel like you're having to justify him and his actions to everyone around you?

I encourage you to read this book...whatever your age or gender! You will come away—if not transformed in your beliefs and understanding—at least more aware that life can be transformed by how you perceive the concept of a rugged gentleman, and how you would choose to change the world by raising one!

~ Avery Austin

THIS BOOK INSPIRED me! I liked how the author stressed the fact that we all need to develop young men to be tough and successful. Being a coach for over two decades, I have seen the attitude of players and parents transform from the "privilege" to play—to one of utter entitlement. Not everyone gets a trophy—in sports or in life—and this author shows "life" has to be worked for.

This is a must read for those in coaching or anyone working with young boys in any aspect. I truly wish I had read this prior to starting my own coaching career and being a better role model as a parent for my own son. After reading Permission to Be Tough, I have taken strategies I learned from this astute author and have incorporated them in my current coaching philosophy; I am seeing results already! Thank you, Tim Austin, for taking the time to write this valuable manuscript and for living into a sense of your purpose in life.

~ Nick Gonzales

Athletic Coach | Gooding, ID

PERMISSION TO BE TOUGH

RAISING BOYS TO BE RUGGED GENTLEMEN

By Tim Austin

Permission to be Tough! Raising Boys to be Rugged Gentlemen
By Tim Austin

Copyright © 2018-2019 Tim Austin

ISBN: 13 978-1-7341670-0-9

Also, in Kindle digital format.
https://www.amazon.com/dp/B081RCL4MJ/

Published by:

7 Horse Press

2719 W Nido Avenue
Mesa, AZ 85202

Ordering Information:

Quantity sales. Special discounts are available on quantity purchases by corporations, associations, and others. For details, contact the publisher at the address above.

Cover by Voices in Print

Edition: 10 9 8 7 6 5 4 3 2 1
Printed in the United States of America

DEDICATION

TO ALL THE LOST BOYS...

We behave as the world teaches us. Our culture is teeming with boys in beards—thirty-year-old teenagers—entitled millennials, violent gang members, uninspired young men, and lost boys. The effects of feminism, absent fathers, computer screen parenting, dependence on government programs and overcrowded classrooms have come to fruition. Change comes from the inside out, thus the world can change—one heart, soul, mind, and body at a time.

It is my observation that many in our culture fell into the blame, entitlement, and anger trap. I beg the question: "Isn't it time we take responsibility for our thoughts and actions?" If WE change, the WORLD will change. It is more effective to look at how we mess up, accept it, look for alternative methods, make changes and get on the right track. Our plight, our position in life, our circumstances are our own responsibility to change if we don't like them.

I hope this book will change the reader and inspire new behavior. My own behavior was changed through pain and heartache. I traveled a rough road; I said and did things that hurt my fellow man. Only recently have I understood the arrogance and contempt legalistic religious training instilled deep in my heart and soul. This book is not about pointing a finger of blame or accusation at anyone. My goal is to bring the reader along to a realization of a problem our society faces, and to make possible suggestions, share ideas and solutions in an effort to encourage new choices or approaches to a growing problem. The motive of this book is to point gently a new direction... the reader taking a new direction, which will enable young men to be the best they can be and in the long run...benefit us all.

The final test of a gentleman is his respect for those who can be of no possible service to him.

~ William Lyon Phelps

TABLE OF CONTENTS

FOREWORD

WHAT DOES IT mean to be a man?

At some point every young male asks this question. Why wouldn't he? It is at the very core of his humanity and identity. However, in modern times it seems that everyone is afraid to answer the question, or the answer is so subjective to feelings or fad that it has lost any real meaning. It has even gotten to the point that society at large is now communicating that there is no such thing as true gender. It is whatever one "identifies with."

As a result, manhood is being lost and there is an identity crisis across the landscape of our nation. Add to that the reality of trying to parent during this time and the burden feels heavier; it seems that there is no way out. I've struggled with this personally. As a pastor for over twenty years and raising two boys, I can say without reservation that I need some help here.

My parents are divorced. My dad left when I was eight and I was raised by a single mom. I went through my formational years, adolescence, and puberty with no male presence in the house. My mom is an amazing woman, but if it were not for some men in the church who walked along side me during this time and gave me some direction on what it means to be a godly man I don't know where I'd be today.

Now I have a family of my own. My wife and I are raising two boys and, like you, we are facing all the challenges of the modern world. Pornography has never been more accessible. The most popular music among teenagers objectifies women and promotes violence. Cell phones, video games and television keep our kids glued to screens.

I know, from experience, my boys can do life online, but am I preparing them to do life in person? In all of this I want my boys to grow into excellent men. I want them to be both tough and tender and to have the wisdom to know how to love and lead well. I want to prepare them for what lies ahead. I want my boys to be rugged gentlemen.

There's hope! I'm grateful for Tim Austin and this crucial work on raising boys to become excellent men. Information helps us, but application changes us. What I found most helpful in what you're about to read is Tim not only gives us the destination of manhood, he tells us HOW to lead our boys there. He provides us a map and coaches us along the way.

Look! There are no perfect parents because there are no perfect people. We all need help and I know this book will help you as it has helped me. I'm taking a moment right now to pray for you and for the boys you're raising. If you don't mind, maybe you could pray for me and my boys too.

Praying for You,
Chad Moore
(October 7, 2019)

PREFACE

WE LIVE IN troubled times, and at some level, we as parents must assume a certain level of responsibility for a common endemic of an entitlement mentality, which breeds a pattern of behavior not acceptable. We desperately seek answers and solutions for events such as school shootings—actions where seemingly ordinary young men chose extra-ordinary actions as a way to express themselves. There is no clear profile for which to monitor social outcasts, bullying, untreated mental illness, or even abusive parenting.

Instead, we tend to look for normalcy, and perhaps even seek to empathize with these marginalized young men...perhaps out a sense of guilt for somehow failing them. These kids are suffering, and often until it is too late, we don't recognize it. We probably see them as normal kids with friends who participate in school activities. How then, do we explain the journals with pages and pages of feeling wronged, being mistreated in life, and "pushed" to complete some horrific act—to meet some unmet need. Studies show the expansion of this sense of aggrieved entitlement and how it exacerbates many of the problems with youth who feel their needs are unique and more important than the needs of those of the society in which they exist.

Do we, in reality, fail them by allowing expectations, which are not within the boundaries of reality?

Do we fail them each time we sweep under the rug problems that may surface because the role of parenting takes too much time or attention?

Do we inadvertently place too much emphasis on—or allow too much demand for—being the center of attention in life?

We must also deal with a social environment surrounding a "me too movement." There is talk about respect for women, and setting boundaries for social, professional, and dating interactions, which requires parents to question early on just what we are going to do to ensure our boys are raised to respect others. As parents, our actions must be intentional and practical, and incorporated into raising tough boys—rugged gentlemen.

This book will not answer all the questions that surface in our parenting. I do trust it to open the awareness of simple things, which when done daily, and with a hefty dose of love, will become a starting point to recreate a society determined to develop a healthy mentality of empathy as we learn to fight a growing society rife with self-centered, potentially narcissistic adults. I intend to build an awareness of what lies before us if we continue to turn our heads and to participate in developing a new attitude: proudly show we focus more on the kind of children we are leaving the world, than the world we seek to leave them.

ACKNOWLEDGMENTS

WRITERS ARE INSPIRED... by events in their lives, by elements of nature, and by people who impact or influence their lives. I am honored to acknowledge those who inspired me to publish *Permission to be Tough: Raising Boys to Be Rugged Gentlemen.*

An incredible friend inspired me...

Over a decade ago I wrote a manuscript that was borne out of my love of parenting, coaching, frustration with parents of my athletes, and a personal road of discovery, which took me from arrogance, contempt, anger and frustration to grace, mercy, forgiveness, kindness, respect and love. The journey was really a recitation of the many things I learned while parenting three awesome kids. I put the manuscript on the shelf where it sat for 10 years as I moved on with life.

Through unbelievable events with Shirley Baer—that included broken bones, carrying her injured body for hours in the mountains, flat tires, malfunctioning car jacks, dogs, surgeries, and long road trips—we had many hours to discuss and share life stories. Along the way, the topic of an old manuscript came to the fore and I satisfied Shirley's curiosity by forwarding a copy to her.

What happened in her life over the following months was astounding. Shirley's 19-year-old son Troy—who was living at home, had stopped attending school, was using electronics late into the night, holding minimum wage jobs, without a car, and appeared seemingly without direction—slowly came around. Troy cleaned up his life, found an apartment, secured gainful employment, and transformed from a boy into a fine young man. Troy, at 23, is currently taking classes and employed with Apple—a young man's dream job.

During this time, Shirley hatched a plan to get the manuscript published, changed her career, and pushed *Permission to be Tough* to completion.

Without her open-minded approach to her son... he might still be directionless, frustrated, and uninspired.

Without her vision... a manuscript would still be sitting on a shelf. It was Shirley's enthusiasm, pure-heartedness, inspiration, energy, and creativity that drove this project.

My deepest heartfelt gratitude goes to this wonderful woman. Thank you, Shirley.

Coach Miller inspired me...

My childhood was an exasperating experience. Starting in 7th grade, my life was touched by a history teacher who was also a coach. Every now and then a kind word or acknowledgment of another person can change a life... save a life. Coach Miller was just that for me.

He was the first person to ever give me a fair shake. I didn't ask for favors or preferential treatment, just fairness. In the sport of wrestling it is quite simple to determine the best athlete. Put your toe on the line and blow the whistle. The truth is quickly and easily discovered, head to head, mano-a-mano, one-on-one. A coach's favorite is irrelevant. Aggression and toughness will eventually win the day.

One spring weekend, Coach drove three of his worst wrestlers two hours to a tournament—just to get us more experience. After a series of quick and decisive losses he drove us back home. What we could count on was that Coach recruited all newcomers. Popularity at school, status of a kid's family, or current lack of ability meant little to him. Coach Jess Miller was the kind of coach who could take a kid who couldn't win a match in Junior High to winning a state championship in High School. That kid was me.

Coach, I want you to know how much I appreciate your help and inspiration. May this book inspire many to do the same for some other young man. May your legacy live on through written words here as I honor how you inspired me to write without even knowing it.

My Uncle Harry inspired me...

When I was a child, my family left the beautiful rolling hills and farm country of northwest Tennessee and moved to the rugged mountains of Colorado. The separation from extended family was tough, and I soon lost track of many relatives.

After college, one of those relatives, my Uncle Harry Austin, became part of my life again. He always had time for me. This man always had an encouraging word. He always understood; he never condemned and was a wonderful friend through very tough times—through years of caring for my grandmother, my kid's events, his divorce, successes, failures, and then my divorce, and countless other life twists and turns—my Uncle Harry was decent to me.

It was this man who taught me a great deal about humility, kindness, empathy, sympathy, thinking of others, and serving others well. He imparted the value of how uplifting a positive attitude is, how important gratitude is in all circumstances, and he impressed upon me to overlook the shortcomings of others without contempt or anger.

Harry, I appreciate you more than words can express. Thank you for helping me be a better person; the person who has courage enough to use a love of writing to convey so many of your life lessons to others responsible for loving and mentoring young men...to be rugged gentlemen.

INTRODUCTION

PARENTING IS A tough job; kids don't come with instruction booklets! We are living in a social environment that tends to create more feelings of entitlement than respect and boundaries. When it comes to raising sons, the process must include a certain amount of "intentional" actions to teach sons to be gentlemen...in practical ways that fall into the parameters of the age-old saying, "Children learn from what they live."

Manners, consideration, kindness, concern and caring for others; the list can look extensive and exhaustive. But you've got this—you can do it! The world as we know it—and the world in which your son will live—comes down to individual family dynamics that influence how your son will ultimately demonstrate courteous and respectful behavior. You play the most significant part in setting the standard reflective of being a gentleman and participate in raising a new and better generation of honorable men.

This book has been written to help parents of future young men develop a human with manners, kindness, responsibility, and empathy toward others. Not only does the rest of the world benefit from your efforts, but the child gets a gigantic boost in self-confidence. In these pages, you will probably see yourself and how you were "managed" during your formative years. Some of that you will want to repeat; there will be other parenting skills you know from personal experience don't work. The primary challenge is to keep your mind open to possibilities—and your heart open to fully loving your son through all manner of life events you can use as "teaching points."

Let's start with expectations! The journey you take with your boys is just that—a journey. What you expect of a one-year-old is significantly different than the actions more capable of a six-year-old, or of those whom you help thrive during the troublesome teen years.

Age is not the only defining element; your son's interests, abilities and personality must be taken into consideration, as well. It is well and good to have a 'playbook' to use as a guideline, but you will have to tweak how you deliver the training, dependent on whether he is shy and quiet—or outgoing and talkative. The idea here is not to pressure a square kid into a round personality; your task is to take the miracle with which you've been blessed and polish it.

> Your task is to take the miracle with which you've been blessed and polish it.

The pages of this book are intended to provide you with a broadened perspective on traits such as empathy, consideration, social skills, communication, sensory expressions, teamwork, accountability...

Some of the profound questions a boy needs help answering with your input are: Do you know your limits? Do you know what you can achieve in life? Are you ready for this kind of adventure?

Until your son tests and pushes beyond those limits... he may never know what he can achieve. Until your son attempts things he has never done, he will never discover what he can accomplish in life. This book might become the new definition of what an adventure is—an adventure with your child.

Although this is a short book, my intention is not for it to be a buzz read—you know the kind about which I am talking. You quickly get through the pages, and as you put it on the shelf, you think to yourself, that was a pretty cool book, but you don't take the time to internalize it or act on the message the writer wanted. You see, for a book to have "sticky-ness" the reader must engage at a deeper level; they should stop, think, and apply the message to their own life. To make this happen for you, you will find several questions that will allow you to get to know yourself—as you are now—and perhaps as you would like, someday, to be.

Although the issue we address in this book is about parenting and the focus is on the children we seek to impact, the process begins at home; it starts with you. Take your time with this book and the myriad questions designed to engage you in a transformation, which makes you the best parent for which those boys could ask. When you know the answers for yourself—consider how much more easily you will be able to get sons on the same path!

Who are you?

What makes you tick?

What yearnings do you have deep inside?

Until you step out in courage and endure a wide array of experiences, you may never figure out who you are. Inside of you is a priceless human spirit, a heart that longs for a new journey. A being with the immense capacity for respect and honor, you are a person who seeks adventure. You will find the answers to questions many parents face—both for themselves and the children they guide through life:

Why am I stuck in this painful situation?

Why can't I seem to break through?

Until a person faces individual weaknesses, there is never room for growth and change. Until failures are admitted and personal responsibility taken, there will never exist sufficient humility to change. Facing reality and facing yourself is how you start your adventure.

Where do I belong?

Where am I going?

Where will I end up?

Until you accept your place in life and accept the challenge to live life to the fullest, you may never know where you belong. Until you own up to your commitments and responsibilities, you may not know where you need to be. Right where you are is where you need to start your adventure.

What is your purpose in life?

Why are you here on this earth at this moment?

Until you wrestle with tough questions, attempt demanding activities, search inside yourself, humbly listen, diligently learn, develop enduring character and deep faith, you may never know your purpose for being here. Right now, is when you need adventure.

Do you have what it takes?

Do you measure up?

Can you hack it?

Until you push your limits, you will never know if you have what it takes. Until you test yourself—and pass that test to your satisfaction—you will never know if you measure up. Until you run a race, you will never know if you have what it takes to hack it, which is why you need adventure.

Raising Boys to be Rugged Gentleman will help you discover HOW.

PERMISSION TO BE TOUGH

RAISING BOYS TO BE RUGGED GENTLEMEN

Permission to be Tough
Raising Boys to be Rugged Gentlemen
Tim Austin

SECTION I

---

*Anyone can be heroic from time to time, but a
gentleman is something you have to be all the time.*

~ Luigi Pirandello (1867-1936)
Italian dramatist, novelist, poet, and short story writer
whose greatest contributions were his plays.

Permission to be Tough
Raising Boys to be Rugged Gentlemen
Tim Austin

CHAPTER 1
WHAT IS A RUGGED GENTLEMAN?

I think the most important thing I have done in my life is to raise two boys.

~ Robert Fogel (1926-2013) American Historian.

A RUGGED GENTLEMAN is that...rugged and gentlemanly. He is prepared and able to handle himself with power and grace all at the same time. In real life, a Rugged Gentleman could walk out of a gym after kicking the snot out of an opponent in an ultimate fighting bout but then take the arm of a little old lady trying to cross the icy street. These should not be considered as incompatible concepts—or perceived as mutually exclusive character traits. Both ruggedness and gentleness found in the same package; a real man has both.

A Rugged Gentleman is healthy and full of life. He eats healthy food, exercises, and gets the proper amount of sleep. He reads good books, converses with intelligent people, views good movies, and continually acquires knowledge.

Permission to be Tough
Raising Boys to be Rugged Gentlemen
Tim Austin

The Rugged Gentleman guards his heart and mind and allows only healthy information to come in. He spends time together with inspiring people, pushes himself, participates in challenging activities, deepens his character, and always tries to do the right thing. He feeds his soul with healthy spiritual messages, develops deep faith, learns to stay steady in difficult times, humbly serves his fellow man and reverently worships his Creator.

Is he perfect?

No, but then, being a Rugged Gentleman is not about perfection. Everyone messes up in life. Instead of dwelling on mistakes and wallowing in self-loathing, a Rugged Gentleman forges ahead and keeps his eyes on the goal of becoming a man of character and honor. While some people insist on focusing on rules, laws, lawbreakers, subverting the law, obeying laws, mistakes, punishment, and consequences, the Rugged Gentleman has a much higher calling. He is in pursuit of respect, honor, and character. Like a profound landmark on a distant mountain, the Rugged Gentleman fixes his gaze, chooses his path, and resolutely forges on toward the prize.

> ...being a Rugged Gentleman is not about perfection.

The aim of Raising Boys to Be Rugged Gentlemen is simple: help develop boys into well-rounded, healthy men. The term *well-rounded* would be a good description of a Rugged Gentleman. In this context the word refers to a

Permission to be Tough
Raising Boys to be Rugged Gentlemen
Tim Austin

person with general knowledge on many subjects, broad common sense, a deep understanding of the essential things of life, self-control, humility, compassion, and an inexhaustible wealth of wisdom. A well-rounded man is adept at many of the harsh and dirty parts of life as well as the refined and beautiful. He may dig a sewer ditch one day and dance with the daughter of a king the next. He may field dress an elk one day and address the Board of Directors the next. He can intelligently discuss an array of topics across a full field of disciplines: microbiology and astronomy, submarine design or the mechanics of climbing Mt. Everest, geology and neurosurgery, the harshness of Antarctica and the warmth of the tropics, the awesome power of nuclear energy and the new possibilities of renewable energy.

The Rugged Gentleman is expected to be great at rough, robust activities—but also taught to be equally skilled in the social graces and etiquette. He might have become proficient in tough sports like football or wrestling but might also be excellent at chess or guitar.

A Rugged Gentleman is a lifetime learner, a humble servant, a seeker of wisdom, a worshipper of his Creator, and an honorable person. He helps, grows, learns, changes, thinks, tries new things, and is courageous and leads others honorably. He is a man of deep character and refreshing wisdom.

Permission to be Tough
Raising Boys to be Rugged Gentlemen
Tim Austin

CHAPTER 2
SPOILED ROTTEN

―――――∞―――――

Life asks not merely what you can do; it asks how much can you endure and not be spoiled?

~ Harry Emerson Fosdick (1878-1969)
American Clergyman.

―――――∞―――――

BOYS, WHEN NOT properly socialized into a family or to respect the hierarchy of a family, will often have a warped sense of who they are. If allowed to dictate the agenda or function of a family, a young lad thinks he is in charge, because...he is in charge. A six-year-old boy is not qualified to manage a family. Several examples exist in nature that may shed light on this concept. One example is that of a wolf pack. Imagine what would happen if a six-month-old pup suddenly decides he is in charge of the pack. I need not further explain through this analogy—the idea is too ridiculous. When parents bow to the temper tantrums, demands, orders or manipulation of a six-year-old, it is

Permission to be Tough
Raising Boys to be Rugged Gentlemen
Tim Austin

equivalent to allowing the child to oversee the family. Neither puppies nor children are qualified to be "leaders of the pack."

Organizations work more efficiently when everyone knows and accepts their place in the hierarchy. Human leaders, like the alpha male of the wolf pack, handle their members and typically have more accountability and duties than their subordinates; their ultimate job is to serve the organization or "pack."

To properly socialize a child into the family structure there are only two choices. A boy is either:

1) in charge of a family, or he is
2) submitted to the hierarchy.

If your child is respectful and understands the hierarchy of your family, you might say, "I am honored to know such a child." However, if he or she is disrespectful and usurps the authority of his parents, it may subject them to overhearing a much different message, "I don't want to have anything to do with your precious little prince!" But I trust that the traffic cops, drill sergeants or prison wardens will eventually have to curb any self-indulgent behavior.

SAY YES TO NEEDS

Give a child everything he needs, and a little bit of what he wants. Kids need meat, potatoes, and vegetables; they don't need Lucky Charms, Cheetos, and Gummy Bears. Kids need nutritious food, good books, adequate clothing, and a safe place to live; they don't need an Xbox, sports cars, and

Permission to be Tough
Raising Boys to be Rugged Gentlemen
Tim Austin

electronic gadgetry. Kids need love, warmth, kind words, validation, affection, and to be treated with respect and dignity; they don't need trophies every time they have a successful bowel movement, medals for doing their math homework or ovations for putting their clothes in the hamper. Kids need a challenge, purpose, and vision for their lives; what they don't need is self-indulgence, flattery, and immediate gratification in everything they attempt.

Give a child everything he needs, and a little bit of what he wants.

~ Dr. Chris Austin, Ph.D.

Just say no when a child wants extraneous stuff.

Say no to frivolous requests; children are too young to know the difference.

However, say yes to books, musical instruments, tools, knowledge, understanding, wisdom, time, help, confidence, clarity, guidance, education, ideas, skills, sports equipment, and healthy food.

It is my personal experience and belief that the most significant errors parents make when raising boys is to destroy their incentive. To give a boy everything he wants, or rescue him from tough situations, mistreat him, shield him from pain or harshly criticize him are obvious ways to destroy his will. This world is a competitive place. Boys need to learn to compete. They need the incentive to want to

Permission to be Tough
Raising Boys to be Rugged Gentlemen
Tim Austin

learn, grow, improve, and become something better than they are today. Otherwise, laziness and stupidity become a habit.

Boys need to learn to win, and they need to learn how to handle losing. To orchestrate false wins or push a boy to compete only when he knows he will enjoy an easy victory, is harmful to his mental and emotional development. There is nothing wrong with losing. To use failure as a reason to blame others and shift focus from what may—in reality—create a lack of awareness about a boy's deficiency and weakness. Conversely, failure can be more effective when used as a motivator for improvement. The approach the parent takes in relation to loss is usually the approach the child will learn.

A boy must find an incentive to learn, earn, grow, become, change, and adapt to his world. Through these things, he can find goals and dreams that motivate; other times pain and failure provide incentive. Wants, wishes, and purpose provide the impetus for some kids. Money and possessions motivate many others. In most cases some passion or hunger inside a young boy's heart drives him to succeed; to give a child everything he wants can destroy inspiration. Most men, by nature, are lazy and detached. This statement is not an attack or an insult; it is just the way most of us are hard-wired. Inventors knew the value of TV remote controls, recliners, and hammocks. Men love to sit on our butts.

CHAPTER 3
FORGET THE VILLAGE—RAISE YOUR KID

It is easier to build strong children than to repair broken men.

~ Fredrick Douglass (1817-1895)
American Author.

MY INTENTION IS not to sound "preachy" throughout this book, but to impress upon our society the responsibility of parents to raise, provide for, educate, teach, discipline, and coach their kids. In a fast-paced crazy world we did not create, it is often necessary to request help from schools, extended family, churches, teachers, coaches, and neighbors to get that job done correctly. But the fact remains, it is our responsibility to make sure our children have all the life skills necessary to become an independent adult and productive member of society.

Many parents have let themselves off the hook by delegating responsibility for their children to others. Also,

Permission to be Tough
Raising Boys to be Rugged Gentlemen
Tim Austin

many parents then demand that some surrogate teach their kid and coach him only in the parent-approved manner. What the parent is inadvertently saying is, "Don't hold him to standards. Don't discipline little Johnny in any way that could bruise his tender ego or diminish his inflated self-esteem. Don't enforce rules or place restrictions on my precious angel."

No matter how qualified you believe others may be at assisting the process, it is the parents' job to make sure the child learns and grows—no one else can fill that role like a parent.

For example, you may send your kids to school with the assumption it is the school's responsibility to teach your kids, and it is. But it is your responsibility to make sure they learn what the teacher presents.

It may be, in part, your church's role to introduce moral, spiritual, and ethical teachings. But it is parents who must model the desired behavior and continually push children to meet the standard of conduct that will help them later in life. It is the parent's job to make sure the child lives a moral, ethical, and spiritual life.

A great coach can teach sportsmanship, a good attitude, and the recreational benefit of sports. A responsible parent must back it up by reinforcing the coach's philosophies, pushing their child to maintain the right attitude, and to provide opportunities to take part in the sport.

To send our children to daycare and expect minimum-wage care-providers to teach them manners, respect and essential social skills is a folly. It is a parent's responsibility

Permission to be Tough
Raising Boys to be Rugged Gentlemen
Tim Austin

to model those skills—to live them—and then send a child to daycare or school to practice what they've seen at home.

Students can gain knowledge and skills in college; however, it is equally important for parents to teach how to apply those skills and guide them towards becoming part of a productive workforce.

Unfortunately, too many parents delegate even the fundamental responsibilities to raise their children to others—for 18 years or more—and then are shocked and horrified to find their kids addicted, pregnant, unemployed, and angry... and wonder why.

PARENTS, PLEASE!

Don't get frustrated with the schools, churches, and colleges if your children are all screwed up. Ultimately, it is your responsibility to provide for your child, not the government's job. Although this is a tough message to deliver, it is genuine and meaningful, "If you leave it up to institutions and governments to raise your kid... you will have a screwed-up kid—guaranteed."

BERT'S STORY

I tell the story of an abusive and disrespectful "public servant" I knew while in high school. As a school superintendent, his legal and ethical lapses were many and varied, but he rarely got caught. He wielded such political power in the school district that, with the help of the teacher's union, he could hand pick any school board member he wanted and pull the proper strings to get them

Permission to be Tough
Raising Boys to be Rugged Gentlemen
Tim Austin

elected. He ran roughshod over anyone who dared stand in his way.

Unfortunately, his son, Bert, was a chip off the old block. Teachers at the school were afraid to discipline or correct Bert for fear of facing the wrath of his father. Bert would cut class anytime he felt like it—and sadly, he suffered no immediate consequences. While cutting class, he would go out and drink beer with his buddies and subsequently show up drunk for football practice. The teachers and coaches dared not do anything about it. Bert would bring beer to school-sponsored events and nary was a word ever said. The recalcitrant young man even got his freshman girlfriend pregnant and had her shuffled off in silence; he had the problem handled in such a manner no consequences came his way.

His dad gave Bert everything but required nothing in return. The young man never learned to display respectful behavior, a helpful attitude, or appreciation for anything. Oh! He had nice cars, fancy clothes, pocket money, cushy jobs at the school district, and college education all at the taxpayers' expense. Very few people respected the father—not even his political "cronies;" very few people appreciated Bert—just his drinking buddies.

For decades following high school, Bert remained the arrogant, disrespectful cad he had been in school. He was rude and disrespectful to people who couldn't help him in some way. The only time he ever showed any respect to anyone was when he wanted something from them—a respect others saw for what it really was, manipulation.

Permission to be Tough
Raising Boys to be Rugged Gentlemen
Tim Austin

There is genuinely merit to the phrase, "Children learn what they live." Just as Bert's father showed contempt and disrespect to the taxpayers, school district employees and ultimately the students in the district, his son displayed horrible disrespect to everyone around him. The father passed disrespect and contempt down to the son. Only time will tell if Bert can ever learn to be polite and decent to his fellow man.

So far, in his mid-50's it doesn't look good. Bert has been through two marriages, doesn't have much to do with his kids, and treats most people with contempt—unless you are someone who can do something for him.

THE TENDENCY TO HOVER

It is important to facilitate, encourage, and oversee your child's development, but don't hover. The dad who completes his son's science fair project and the mom who scrutinizes every word and deed of her son's coach both are examples of hovering parents. Don't do it. Your boys need to try - and fail - to learn how to complete a project. They need to have the experiences, which teach him how to handle adults who treat him differently than his parents treat him. It is just a part of life.

Hovering parents often want to control every aspect of their kid's lives. At some point, you must give it up. You can't control your children. And you shouldn't navigate them out of every tight spot. If you continue to hover, your result will be a rebellious, angry, or dependent young man on your hands.

Permission to be Tough
Raising Boys to be Rugged Gentlemen
Tim Austin

In fifth grade, my son completed a school project that was clever and cute, but it looked like a fifth grader had done it! However, when he took it to school and sat it beside the other projects—completed by dads who were professional millworkers, furniture makers, pipe fitters, ornamental iron artisans, interior designers, and painters—his project looked pathetic. But it was his, and he was proud of it! The other kids didn't give a hoot about their projects. They didn't appear to have learned anything.

However...

My son had learned many things...he learned a little about woodworking, painting, electricity, and using tools. He also learned responsibility, tenacity, and patience—and how to research—as he figured out two baffling problems that surfaced during the project. My son got high marks on the project... but through the experience, he gained confidence, experience, and skills the other kids missed.

My advice is not to micromanage or hover. Start the process to let go of your son; let him try—and fail—at different activities. Let him learn through experience as you stand back...guide and coach. The goal of raising boys is not to eliminate all risks... it is to guide and teach your son to develop a deep character, wisdom, skill, and experience which are often the product of a willingness to take on risk.

RISK MANAGEMENT

Kids best learn to manage risk and caution by pushing the limits and making mistakes. It is far better if they make small mistakes, so they can develop sufficient wisdom and

Permission to be Tough
Raising Boys to be Rugged Gentlemen
Tim Austin

judgment when attempting new activities and projects. It is far better for parents to help kids learn to test limits gradually vs. going hog wild into danger—with no skills or reference point. The following story is a fitting example.

A youngster who resided in our neighborhood built a go-cart looking contraption out of a skateboard. Being creative, he figured out how to lie down on it and steer by leaning. Unfortunately, rather than testing it on smaller hills he took his first ride on a long, very steep street! Sadly, with just a tiny bit more wisdom, he would have known better. Scraping his broken and mangled body from the curb at the bottom of the hill was a very unpleasant task for the EMTs. Although learning to push the limits a little at a time is a good thing for a boy to learn—to FIRST develop the skills to correctly assess risk and have the wisdom to avoid monumental mistakes is priceless.

Let me ask you a fundamental question,

"Are you raising your kid to do every task perfectly in life—or are you growing a healthy, well-adjusted young man?"

I ask, primarily to open your mind and heart, to the impact to try to teach your kid to be perfect. If that is your intention, then—by all means—hover and micromanage his life. However, if your preference is to grow a courageous young man, back off and let him, well—grow!

Permission to be Tough
Raising Boys to be Rugged Gentlemen
Tim Austin

CHAPTER 4
MOM'S ROLE:
TO INSPIRE AND NURTURE

―――――∽∽―――――

If you bungle raising your children, I don't think
whatever else you do matters very much.

~ Jackie Kennedy (1929-1994)
America First Lady.

―――――∽∽―――――

BOYS AND GIRLS alike need nurturing, kindness, softness, gentleness, and sweetness during the early years of life. There is no substitute for a mom's role in providing the soft and gentle side of life to a young boy. But at some point, the need for the sweet and kind mommy role decreases as boys look to a father's ruggedness, toughness, and courageous persona. If the mom hangs onto the primary parenting role and continues to coddle a teenage boy, she will probably meet with resistance by the boy... or she may raise a wimpy, sweet, dependent momma's boy. And if she does, other kids will probably point out to her son just what a wimp he is!

Permission to be Tough
Raising Boys to be Rugged Gentlemen
Tim Austin

Teenagers are rarely kind when they point out the deficiencies of others!

Let me tell you a story about a boy whose stepmom thought it was cute that her teenage stepson was very effeminate, sweet, sensitive, and emotional. It was an openly stated goal in raising her stepson. Before she came into the picture... the boy was a strong, courageous young lad. The dad was compliant and allowed the mom to apply her skill of emasculation. Regrettably, by the time he reached high school, the boy was an emotional train wreck. He was cute, sweet, sensitive, and weak; he sounded like a girl, walked like a girl, socialized only with girls, and acted like a girl. He earned no respect from boys. He also later experienced confusion over his sexual identity because he didn't know who or what he was.

Moms, this message is especially for you: I urge you to resist the temptation to cling to the primary parenting role to nurture and insist on sweetness and sensitivity from your boy—at the exclusion of toughness and courage. A boy needs to be sweet and sensitive in some situations, but he also needs to be rugged and tough enough to learn how to be a protector and provider. I implore you to push him toward his dad or other strong, respectable men.

If I could speak openly with every loving mother in America, I would say, "Keep in mind, you are a natural nurturer. When you continually encourage your son to handle life's problems using feminine strategies, sadly, you may hinder his development as a man."

Permission to be Tough
Raising Boys to be Rugged Gentlemen
Tim Austin

SINGLE MOMS

As I progress through this minefield, please understand that it is with caution, humility, and trepidation I do so. I don't want a misunderstanding to turn anyone away from the core message of this book. Women, abandoned and abused by pathetic men, don't want to hear anything more from another man commenting on their struggles and their plight. I understand and accept that. However, I beg you to read on for the sake of your son's well-being.

Let me be the first to affirm what you are doing... to hang in there and fight for your kids. Your man let you down—and probably messed up your life and your kids' lives. As a fellow citizen, I want to say, "Thank you for doing what you can to raise healthy children as well-adjusted adults and productive citizens who are not in jail."

We both know with the greatest certainty you would not think of abandoning your kids the way your mate did, so I would also state, "My hat is off to you. Please, take no condemnation or blame from my words!"

Later in this book, I outline dozens of activities that can help boys to learn what it is to be a Rugged Gentleman. Moms can plan and take part in the activities with their sons, and the boys will benefit from that experience. But the fact remains... a boy needs a respectful man to model healthy male behavior. Every boy genuinely needs a first-rate man; one who is ready to lend courage, strength, righteousness, respect, knowledge, and affirmation to the youngster. Boys need strong, healthy men; the more time they can spend with Rugged Gentlemen, the more likely they will catch the

Permission to be Tough
Raising Boys to be Rugged Gentlemen
Tim Austin

required traits in their own lives. To learn the identifying characteristics of such a man, check out my book, *Real Men Don't Talk Trash: The Essential Guide to Being a First-Rate Man.*

HELP WITH RAISING BOYS

Single moms must be creative and resourceful to make it in the world. The following suggestions call on you to use that resourcefulness and creativity to get your son the help with these needs. These are only suggestions; you may come up with others that are better suited to your situation.

If your son is young, enrolling him in the Cub Scouts and Boy Scouts program is a great place to start. Find a troop led by a strong, healthy, respectful adult male and your son will benefit. Scouting activities are safe, structured, and usually simple—but may still prove to be a challenge for some boys.

Solicit the help of the boy's grandfather if he is a strong, honorable man. Encourage them to engage in some activities listed later in this book. Bolster a relationship between the boy and his grandfather. Help set-up times for them to meet and spend time in activities together.

Ask for help from an uncle, older cousin, or robust and healthy neighbor. Many strong, respectful men are more than willing to help a single mom with her boys. But some things that cross the mind of a man willing to take your son under his wing include:

Will I be sued if this boy gets hurt?

Permission to be Tough
Raising Boys to be Rugged Gentlemen
Tim Austin

Will I be accused of molesting a boy if I discipline him and the boy resents it?

Will I be blamed if I take this kid on an activity and something goes wrong, and someone gets hurt?

Our culture includes millions of level-headed, healthy men of a deep character who could significantly help your son but would never offer or even allow yours along for fear of lawsuits. Over the years, I declined to allow certain of my son's friends to come along, primarily because I knew if anything went wrong, I would be in a lawsuit.

Moms, you must encourage risk. You must convince strong, healthy men—who might teach your son—that you will not seek recourse if the boy gets hurt. I will be honest with you—boys need activities that involve risk.

Every boy needs to learn their limits, understand their abilities, and have the wisdom to know when they are pushing it too far. Translation: "pushing it too far" means doing something beyond their capacity that sometimes gets them hurt.

A boy will never know his limits until he tests them. A good role model will examine your son's limits if you let him. Offer a signed waiver of liability to a good man who might be hesitant to let your son tag along on activities. These can be tough decisions for a protective mom who has a huge heart and tons of compassion. You may have to find courage and support from other moms who have pushed their boys toward tough activities. But it needs to happen for your son to grow up.

Permission to be Tough
Raising Boys to be Rugged Gentlemen
Tim Austin

Moms, I know some of you may find the next paragraph to be unreasonable... but please let me offer a man's perspective!

My boys participate in tough sports. My oldest son ripped his knee out during the middle of his senior year in high school and required repairs of knee parts I can't even pronounce. During the long and painful recovery, the injury motivated him to work hard to get back to the football field—there was a college scholarship at stake. A mom commented one day, "It was just plain crazy to risk another injury!"

My response? "I would have allowed my son to play even knowing with 100% certainty he would rip his knee out! His school, the coaches, fellow players, and even his competitors—the whole program—was absolutely the best experience of his life. I wouldn't have taken that away from him for anything!"

> Every boy carries within his mind some questions for which he needs answers.

And I implore you, moms, to develop a similar attitude with your boys.

It is interesting that physical injuries are usually not fatal. The body can repair itself, but there are emotional injuries that can maim for life. Every boy carries within his mind some questions for which he needs answers.

Permission to be Tough
Raising Boys to be Rugged Gentlemen
Tim Austin

Do I have what it takes?

Am I worthy?

Does my dad believe in me?

Will I ever be able to "measure up" in this world?

Am I strong enough to compete in this world?

Can I hack it?

Boys must answer those questions at some point. How do you want your young man to answer those questions?

When removed from a contact sport to avoid injuries, a boy may hear "You don't have what it takes."

In fact, from a kid's perspective, it's potentially telling him, "You are just not strong enough or tough enough to hack it."

The emotional injury a boy suffers when his parent tells him he doesn't have what it takes to play a sport or tackle some other challenge can debilitate a kid—boys often are not able to put into words their need to measure up—nor do they consciously understand there is a need to do so. They may not bring the issue up for years if ever...but they will have forever been impacted by it.

The travesty, however, remains for life—a subtle and subconscious seed planted: "You don't have what it takes." Even though a child may consent to the "less dangerous" sport he may look back years later and wonder, "Could I have hacked it if they'd believed in me?

Two knee surgeries were a small price to pay for the affirmation, challenge, validation, and courage my son

Permission to be Tough
Raising Boys to be Rugged Gentlemen
Tim Austin

ultimately received from strong, healthy coaches and fellow teammates. The dollars and pain were a small price to pay for the character my son developed. During this time, he could answer many of the burning questions in his life; he put himself through the test. And I am proud to say, "He passed with flying colors. He is a young man of which any dad would be proud."

Single moms, I also beseech you to enroll your son in sports, especially wrestling, martial arts, hockey, or football.

Let him be tough.

Find good coaches who are respectful men.

Explain your predicament and solicit their help.

Let the coach know you will not second guess him or question his authority as he trains your son.

Let the coach challenge him and set high standards for your son.

Let your son get beat up, bruised up and knocked around; it will help him more than you can imagine.

And bite your tongue unless someone does something blatantly harmful and destructive to your kid.

I must tell you from my experience coaching my sons in wrestling, it is extremely hard on a dad to watch his kid get the snot kicked out of him. It is even tougher for a mom to allow a boy to test his abilities against others and test his limits."

A great coach will know how to put his arm around the boy and affirm his value as a human being, encourage more

Permission to be Tough
Raising Boys to be Rugged Gentlemen
Tim Austin

dedicated behavior, and inspire your son to do better. A great coach will answer some of those nagging questions boys face.

Many churches have programs for boys, which teach them a certain ruggedness. Find a good church or civic organization that offers help for single moms and boys. Enroll your son in activities led by strong, respectful men every chance you get.

Some organizations specialize in programs for kids such as the YMCA or Boy's Club. Look for spiritual and faith-based programs—such as AWANA or Royal Rangers—needed by boys. "Moms... be intentional in these selections; use them to help your son find healthy spiritual training... just as you help him with physical, mental and emotional growth activities."

Faith is the greatest need in the life of a young man. With a strong spiritual depth, many boys have been able to survive lack of emotional, mental, and physical support and affirmation from a strong man. I also believe without faith, a young man may find it difficult to develop a deep character—even if he has his physical, mental, and emotional needs met.

Outward Bound and Wilderness Trek are also good examples of reputable organizations that help teenage kids. Whenever you find a program led by strong, healthy men, get your son involved. The program is not nearly as important as the fact it involves a strong leader.

Farmers and ranchers always need laborers. If you live in a rural area, ask a farmer or rancher to help you better

Permission to be Tough
Raising Boys to be Rugged Gentlemen
Tim Austin

raise your son by giving him a job. Rural people are typically the salt of the earth folks; they have the heart to help anyone. However, be respectful, the very last thing country folks need is arrogant city folks coming around telling them what to do or how to live.

Your mother probably taught you to ask for what you want in life. She also showed you that if you don't ask, the answer will always be "no." Take it from my voice of experience, most Rugged Gentlemen I know would be happy to include a boy or two in activities they plan with their son. Every respectful man I am acquainted with would love to take another boy along... and share activities that teach him and ultimately, help the lad out. Take the time to find a:

Strong, healthy dad at your son's school and ask if your son can tag along on activities.

Rugged Gentleman at church and ask if he would willingly help your son.

A co-worker who takes his boys on activities and ask him to let your son tag along.

THE CHALLENGES OF A MOM

Life can often feel overwhelming to most single moms. I understand that time is precious and for you to arrange or organize one more activity for your son may be more than you can stand. But I would implore you to get him the help he needs! Put your heads together with other single moms and gather their ideas. Share contacts with each other when you find strong, healthy coaches, scoutmasters, and other youth leaders.

Permission to be Tough
Raising Boys to be Rugged Gentlemen
Tim Austin

I also understand when a single mother says, "Please, don 't caution me! I am careful in who I solicit to mentor and help my sons. My instinct is to know of the myriad dangers lurking about in our society." There are many predators in this world. Just a few decades ago it was unheard of for men to prey on boys; it is now a cruel reality in our society.

Moms must work up the courage to take risks to provide their sons what they need. Be wise.... be aware. Most men are not predators; however, most men don't feel the freedom to reach out and help youngsters, either. Look at it this way, by asking a strong, respectful Rugged Gentleman to help your son, you may do both a favor.

A FEMININE SIDE

I am troubled by the message I have heard for years—that I am supposed to get in touch with my feminine side. Unfortunately, no one has ever precisely defined what that means. I can't tell if it means being sensitive, kind, and gentle or weak, wimpy, and giving in. In my honest opinion, I have not experienced men having a "feminine" side except when someone robs their masculinity and they feel effeminate and soft. To support my belief, I postulate that masculinity has its form of kindness and gentleness, but it is more in the way of being a protector of the weak and a provider for one's family.

THE ART OF INSPIRING A YOUNG MAN

"Mommy, watch this!" How many times do you hear this from your boys? Why do you suppose they crave your attention? It guarantees your attention and praise to inspire

31

Permission to be Tough
Raising Boys to be Rugged Gentlemen
Tim Austin

any young man; you will discover your words are more precious than gold to his emotional development. Alternatively, you will find your words also have the power to rip his heart to shreds rather than inspire him to heights no man has ever gone before. Your words…

Can be what he builds his life around.

Will shape the life of your boys and young men.

There is little doubt boys need a cheerleader in life.

They need someone who:

Notices and watches them.

Fully appreciates them.

Cheers them on to try new activities, develop a deep character and find the courage to live life with adventure.

Whatever you want a boy to do—whatever you want him to be like—compliment him on it. And by all means, Cheer! Cheer him on as he tries and fails—and tries yet again.

In being a parent, let me share one big, red-flag alert, "Be careful with the power of your words." If you want a boy to care about his appearance—his looks, hair, clothes, or physical characteristics—all it takes are simple, frequent compliments on the way he looks. Over time, what is important to you will naturally morph into what is important to him. Proceed with caution, however. if you compliment him on superficial, shallow attributes of his appearance, he will probably be a shallow young man…

Permission to be Tough
Raising Boys to be Rugged Gentlemen
Tim Austin

fixated continuously on his looks. My suggestion is to compliment him on what is important.

When a young man displays behavior that shows he is developing patience, self-control, compassion, kindness, courage, love, humility, peace, faith, or tenacity—compliment him on that behavior.

Speak your appreciation to him for his willingness to grow and learn in those attributes. If your young man shows signs of creative thinking, toughness, bravery, talent, or respect toward others, compliment him on what you see in his maturity.

Compliment small hints of the behavior of which you want to see more.

Compliment him on attitude, effort, skill, or energy he puts behind a project.

Tell him you believe in him and trust him; tell him you know he can do it.

Tell him he has what it takes to be a great husband someday, and that you know he is.

Tell him he is worthy, strong, and courageous.

When he shows hints that he is developing deep character, tell him you see his progress.

But more than anything—know when you tell a young man you respect him for his character, intellect, ability, and strength—you will see more and more of it!

Moms, especially important... never forget the power of your negative words. Words of criticism, anger, distrust, weakness, blame, failure, and accusation will cut a child to

Permission to be Tough
Raising Boys to be Rugged Gentlemen
Tim Austin

the core. Be generous with your words of admiration, praise, and well-deserved flattery.

In paying attention to the power of negative comments, I cannot state strongly enough, "Don't ever lie to a kid!"

If he messed up a school project, don't tell him how wonderful it is, he will learn you are not trustworthy, and your compliments are meaningless and superficial. However, if a portion of the project was good, tell him so.

> If he put solid effort and thought into his project, tell him so.

> If he was responsible and started and completed the project on time, tell him you noticed and appreciated that about him.

You can always find something positive and good about many accomplishments. The caveat here is to not fall into the trap of feeling like you must give your son a medal and or a congressional citation for every little thing he does. You can inadvertently turn a kid into a "compliment junkie" who seeks adoration every time he finishes eating his cheeseburger. However, if you err, make it on the side of expressing too much adoration in a world that will beat him down.

> Life can be fun and exciting because Moms can...

> Get away with some things a dad can't do. For instance, a mom can periodically get away with flattery and sweet words of adoration that any boy will love to hear. A dad might lose credibility and trust if he tried using similar words.

Permission to be Tough
Raising Boys to be Rugged Gentlemen
Tim Austin

Use words of inspiration and physical touch that most dads wouldn't dare try with his young man.

Get away with certain, well-chosen words of attraction or compliments that would make a boy blush, but similar words from a dad would embarrass him.

Another fascinating element of allowing boys to feel the affection from his mother is that a boy needs to know he is something special, which will someday attract a female. The powerful words of a mom can steer him to develop strong characteristics and give him confidence around the girls. Use words that tell him who he is, what he is, what you appreciate about him and what he is becoming.

Set aside frustration as you try to figure out which compliments will inspire, and which will devastate or ruin your kid. That is why I specifically titled this subsection "The Art of Inspiring a Young Man." If you notice, I didn't call it "The Science..." There is no formula or hard rule of how to master this. It is an art. Fortunately, over time, the better you become at the art, the more your words will lift your young man to heights unknown.

Permission to be Tough
Raising Boys to be Rugged Gentlemen
Tim Austin

CHAPTER 5
DAD'S ROLE
TO AFFIRM AND CHALLENGE

Fathering makes a man, whatever his standing in the eyes of the world, feel strong and good and important, just as he makes his child feel loved and valued.

~ Frank Pittman, 1935-2012
American Psychologist.

ONE OF THE greatest needs in the life of a boy is to have a strong healthy man by his side. Boys need someone to model healthy behavior worthy of emulating. Humans learn best by watching and imitating what they see. Why do you think there are 4,000 instructional videos on improving a golf swing, fielding a baseball, or handling a basketball? If we see it and imitate it, we can learn it. We imitate what we see.

When a mom changes a baby's diaper the 5-year-old daughter changes her baby doll's diaper. When a dad hammers a nail into the wood the 4-year-old-boy will smash

Permission to be Tough
Raising Boys to be Rugged Gentlemen
Tim Austin

his finger 25 times trying to mimic dad. It is natural for young children to copy the actions, words, and attitudes of grown-ups in their lives.

I will always applaud the need for mothers in a boy's life but will never discount the need for a dad.

Boys need their dads, so they have someone to copy. Nothing equals time with a wholesome dad. Something incredible passes between a respectful man and a boy when they do nothing more than spend time together. There is no surprise; boys communicate verbally less than girls; it is just a fact of life. While little girls love to learn by talking and relating to other kids face to face, boys interact shoulder to shoulder as they pretend to simulate what they will experience in the real world. In the good-ole-days when kids played in the dirt, Tonka™ trucks were a smash hit with boys because the little yellow trucks and loaders placed a boy on a major construction site where the boss was expecting the daily quota of loading, hauling and grading done. Boys need playmates in dirt moving situations to ensure someone is there to help meet that daily quota unless you happen to be a big brother. In that case, having a little brother on the site gives you someone to bury, throw dirt on, or blame for the uprooting of flowers!

> It is natural for young children to copy the actions, words, and attitudes of grown-ups in their lives.

Permission to be Tough
Raising Boys to be Rugged Gentlemen
Tim Austin

QUALITY TIME

Not too long ago the concept of "quality time" entered the American vocabulary. The Agrarian age found dads, sons, uncles, cousins, and grandfathers all working in the fields together. The Industrial Age ushered in the need for dads to leave home to work in the factories, which automatically meant less time spent with children. It also meant less knowledge, understanding, attitudes and wisdom being handed from dads to sons. Schools picked up slack in transferring knowledge; however, boys need far more than just knowledge from their dads.

In our culture, dads have tried to convince themselves spending a few minutes of so-called "quality time" with the kids would more than compensate for the lack of a quantity of time. Unfortunately, that has proven not to be true. We now know boys long for and need a good man to copy and that absolutely nothing can make up for the lack of time spent together.

The term "teachable moment" also became a part of our lexicon. This was to identify the salient moments in a child's life when important lessons were shared. Young boys need time with their dads. Value labels are irrelevant to a child. What boys need is time to spend with a healthy man—to watch and copy a healthy male adult. He needs to have a healthy man to listen to and to emulate and transfer ideas and attitudes. A boy also needs a healthy man to discuss important concepts with him.

Permission to be Tough
Raising Boys to be Rugged Gentlemen
Tim Austin

Boys need a dad who will correct unruly behavior, praise good attitudes, and model proper respect and honor toward others.

Just as the Agrarian Age reflected fathers and boys working side by side, and in the Industrial Age men left the home to work. Now, we are in the Information Age, where we see fathers sitting on the couch beside their son—but have no interaction. In some ways, our world is tragic; a world where a boy and his father may live in the same house watching TV—in their respective rooms—and never even see each other, let alone interact.

Besides dads not being "present," perverted men now prey on boys via the Internet as a way to fulfill demented sexual fantasies. Sadly, we know many dads aren't present because at some point they abandoned their families and left the innocent children vulnerable to poverty, crime, and feelings of inadequacy and guilt. The travesty is that after the fathers disappear, they leave single moms to raise boys and do the best they can, with no man around to help caution or ward off dangerous predators.

Our cultural norms have also evolved. Boys grow up in a feminized culture, observing feminine behavior, hearing primarily feminine perspectives, and often watching strong men ridiculed on TV. Boys watch the attack of strong healthy men in the media and they interact little with healthy men— and all the while—we wonder why:

> Our boys are not growing up to be responsible and honorable men.

Permission to be Tough
Raising Boys to be Rugged Gentlemen
Tim Austin

34-year-old boys are in their underwear playing Xbox in their parent's basement mid-day, when they should be out working.

A growing number of our young men don't grow up, go to college, get a job, get married, have kids of their own or have a successful career. These are rites of passage of life being denied them.

Boys often grow up with no strong healthy men to model acceptable behavior. When the prevailing message is that men are idiotic, lazy brutes or cutthroat, ruthless jerks...it is little wonder they ever venture out of the basement!

Both boys and girls need nurturing and to be treated with tender care in the early years of their lives. But as they mature, boys gravitate toward

> To capture the attention of a boy all you need is a pile of rocks, a Tonka truck, a puddle of water, a bucket, or a tree.

other boys and the more rugged elements of their world. To capture the attention of a boy all you need is a pile of rocks, a Tonka truck, a puddle of water, a bucket, or a tree. What looks like play, to the untrained eye, is merely a lad learning particularly important life lessons. Splattering mud on everyone in sight may look like mischief to the world, but in a little man's heart, is a simple educational activity. It is unfortunate that, when a dad hears about it, there may be

Permission to be Tough
Raising Boys to be Rugged Gentlemen
Tim Austin

another painful lesson as well! Lessons learned are sometimes disciplinary measures.

The best guidance you can give your child is to help them develop the self-discipline necessary to be patient, empathetic, and loving. The next time you feel frustrated, stop, and think of how you can shift conflict by validating feelings. Make them aware you are not condoning bad choices or giving in to defiant behavior but listening to and trying to understand them.

I encourage you to consider the possibility: if the only thing dads could do for their sons was to validate them with kind words, provide basic needs, and affirm youngsters with uplifting words—our young men would have a good chance to grow up to and evolve as healthy—mentally, physically and emotionally.

To validate your child is easy. Consider delivering a simple message "Your feelings matter, even if I sometimes don't understand." When you validate a child, your message at least conveys empathy. This can build self-esteem and diminish the defiant behavior. Defiance is the language of children who do not feel understood.

This is a simple concept. Don't, please don't, attempt to make this book more complicated than it is. The concepts are simple—yet are of paramount importance in the life of a young man.

INVESTING time with a boy each day takes on a different connotation than SPENDING time. Think about it! Shoulder to shoulder you teach him life skills as you work side by side. You are investing in a boy's future as a potentially Rugged

Permission to be Tough
Raising Boys to be Rugged Gentlemen
Tim Austin

Gentleman each time you show him how to take care of the home or automobile maintenance, manage school homework, or just hang out together. Each can be profound time—in the mind of a boy. When you take time to speak kind words and affirm a boy's value, it will do wonders for his mental and emotional well-being. As a parent, I consider every minute to be quality time. And this supports another important parenting lesson:

The following includes things a boy desperately needs from his dad or another Rugged Gentleman in his life.

Modeling: Dads can pass down much of what a boy needs just by modeling a respectful, honorable, courageous, and character-filled life. Much of what boys learn is caught rather than taught. Modeling is how dads pass along a legacy without having to say much.

Affirmation: Words are powerful. A boy who hears a word of affirmation each day will grow up to be a strong healthy young man. Just to know a man he admires notices, cares, and expresses his affirmation is powerful in the mind and heart of a boy.

Acceptance: The deep knowing a strong, healthy man accepts you as on the same level as another man is enough to inspire a boy to achieve far more than he ever envisioned for himself. Boys need to know they are acceptable to their dad.

Teaching: Some of what a boy needs to know must be taught. A dad who is a patient teacher is priceless to his son. A wise, teaching parent who says the right words to encourage and affirm does more than just teach the subject

Permission to be Tough
Raising Boys to be Rugged Gentlemen
Tim Austin

at hand. For a boy to learn who and what he is—and to see and embrace his purpose in life—is profound.

Discipline: Most boys, if left to their own internal drive, will produce a tiny fraction of what they are able to produce. Having a strong man around to help a boy discipline his own mind, habits, heart, and behavior will set a lad on the course for success in life. In this same context, it is important to remind parents to not confuse discipline with punishment.

Protection: Security can be a big issue in the mind of a lad as he is growing up. A father who handles his son by using threats, harshness, manipulation, physical harm, unfair treatment, and vicious behavior will quickly cause a boy to lose heart. This harmful treatment pushes a boy away from the person to whom he looks for protection, and puts the child at risk, to become angry, withdrawn, and open to being addicted to unhealthy environments or behaviors. This risk also includes feeling pushed to engage in destructive anti-social behavior. A dad must also protect his sons from bullies and tyrants—or at least coach the boy to take care of the problems himself.

Inspiration: Many boys need the motivation to do a good job in life. Without someone to push us toward a semblance of excellence, our lives would be full of projects partially finished, lessons half studied, fields half plowed, fences half built, and ditches half dug.

Punishment: Let's face it… defiant boys must be—from time to time—appropriately punished to help them associate rebellion with discomfort sufficient for them to understand the consequences. There is evidence to reflect that paternal

Permission to be Tough
Raising Boys to be Rugged Gentlemen
Tim Austin

discipline is more effective than the softness normally administered by the mom. Sometimes boys must suffer painful consequences for disruptive behavior, without which they may not learn to control themselves. For this concept to work, however, and do so from a perspective on health, we must offer a child BOTH A CONSEQUENCE AND FOLLOW THROUGH.

Rebellion: Let me preface this section by noting it is relatively normal that boys naturally sometimes act on ill-conceived ideas, mischief, and foolishness. It is only the most serious behaviors—that beg for a correction—for example, defiance and rebellion. It is a difficult line to walk; it is far too easy to foster contempt and scorn in a boy... if we treat his rebellion as nothing more than a mistake. A child naturally driven to defiance and rebellion may well see evidence of what he perceives as weakness and fear. A defiant lad loves weakness and fear. He masters taking advantage of both.

Sometimes, a caring, loving adult may inadvertently teach a child in the throes of defiance and rebellion, how to bully others physically, mentally, or emotionally to get what he wants. Corrective action is the only way to turn such a child from his unhealthy actions—with sufficient influence to alter his behavior.

If this is how boys think and behave as a general rule, a few corrective swats on the backside now may help him avoid a much more severe punishment some warden may have in store for him at a later time.

It is part of life for boys to make mistakes and learn the most valuable lessons from the natural consequences of

Permission to be Tough
Raising Boys to be Rugged Gentlemen
Tim Austin

their mistakes. Shielding a boy from discomfort and pain caused by his mistakes opens a greater possibility he may continue to make mistakes forever. At some level, a certain amount of pain can be a wonderful thing; focus on the pain that tells us to move our hand before we do horrible damage if we touch a hot stove. Pain motivates us to do what is necessary to avoid future agony.

In much the same way, we can view failure as something positive. It also teaches us what not to do as it steers our children in a more positive direction. It steers a lad in a different direction...it moves him away from things not fitting for his best interest. Later in life, the ability to look at failure from a healthier perspective prevents boys from repeating previous mistakes in their future careers. Failure will test and try them as young boys and, they will have a keen understanding of what they are not well-fitted to do.

We relate to another example where the experience of business failure causes pain. It is little more than a natural mechanism through which it runs inadequately prepared businesspeople out of business. If you teach your son early in life how to apply sound, healthy business practices it is a given there will be unlimited opportunities for him to succeed.

A wise dad will teach a boy in such a way that the lad is eager to turn and model the good behavior instrumental in his own success. A boy who receives respectful affirmation will probably turn and affirm his own kids someday, he will:

Accept them, teach, discipline, protect, inspire, and punish his own children in a rugged, but gentle way.

Permission to be Tough
Raising Boys to be Rugged Gentlemen
Tim Austin

Pass to his son a healthy worldview, and impart good habits, good attitudes, and wisdom.

Show humility, grace, and compassion to his sons and will teach them to respect and serve their fellow man.

Reflect on how high you could have soared if someone had inspired you?

What could you have done that nobody has ever done?

A Rugged Gentlemen leaves a legacy of righteous behavior and faith to his sons.

THE ART OF INSPIRING A YOUNG MAN (TAKE TWO)

Men, let me ask you a few deeply profound and personal questions:

What could you have learned that nobody has ever known if you had some guidance?

What could you have attained that nobody has ever reached had you experienced the inspiration of a strong healthy man behind you?

I ask you to consider these questions, so you might fully understand just how much:

Boys long to have a strong man believe in them and approve of them.

Genuine validation and acceptance are like a launching pad for a kid.

Boys look to a strong man for approval as part of human nature.

Permission to be Tough
Raising Boys to be Rugged Gentlemen
Tim Austin

Once a young man feels your approval, validation, and acceptance he gives himself the permission to go try something new. When withholding that validation and approval, he continually asks the nagging questions:

> Am I okay?
> Do I have what it takes?
> Can I hack it in life?
> Am I smart enough?
> Am I tough enough?

Men, boys look to you for indirect answers to some of these nagging questions! I want to reiterate how careful you must be when telling a boy, "You are great...you look great...you are perfect."

Always keep in mind there is a thin line between genuine approval and this

> Praise a young man and he will naturally gravitate toward becoming that for which you praised him; it is that for which he will strive to improve or strive to become

potentially dangerous formula for the creation of an arrogant young man—should he believe he is superior or somehow positioned at the pinnacle of all mankind!

Instead, learn to focus your praise on his effort and attitude even if he failed at the results he was trying to achieve. There is always room to reaffirm your son, and all that takes is appropriate praise. Your underlying message should convey the ideas and the process used to arrive at what was obviously a well-thought conclusion, even if he's

Permission to be Tough
Raising Boys to be Rugged Gentlemen
Tim Austin

not happy with a result or conclusion he wanted. He still may have earned praise for:

Ability and intellect even if he heads in a different direction in life than you wanted him to go.

Effort and the energy he put into a project even if the project fails.

Work effort when it shows signs of excellence, quality, and skill, even if the work isn't perfect.

Applaudable behavior when he shows signs of learning and practicing patience, kindness, goodness, righteousness, respect, and humility.

.

Permission to be Tough
Raising Boys to be Rugged Gentlemen
Tim Austin

CHAPTER 6
SPORTS
A SNAPSHOT OF LIFE

Sometimes, without effort, you live in the moment.
You don't regret the past or worry about the future,
and in that moment, everything flashes before your
eyes, a clear snapshot of what has to be done, and
everything pauses.

~ *Rebecca McNutt*
Author, Shadowed Skies: The Third Smog City Novel.

GOOD COACHING CAN create a wonderful experience for a young man. Conversely, lousy training can frustrate a youngster or even destroy his will to take part in sports altogether. This chapter was difficult to write; but there are valuable lessons in it:

Boys need to embrace the reality you've discovered: that life is difficult, and no, it is not always what you find comfortable or agreeable; yet you will most likely survive.

Permission to be Tough
Raising Boys to be Rugged Gentlemen
Tim Austin

Boys also need to hear, "There will be instances when you recognize a situation as bullying; it is never right, and you should be ok with taking a stand against it."

The following story will show just what I am trying to convey. It is not a story about me, but one that disturbed me sufficiently to never forget what transpired.

Soon after I graduated high school, the school administrators hired a man to coach football and wrestling who disrespected every athlete he coached. He knew less about football than the intimidation, insults, cruelty, and favoritism he displayed. The team did not fare well; the worst defeat in the history of Colorado high school football is his "glory line."

Physical Education classes looked much like his actions on the football field. The story goes that during PE class the coach set up a kickball game and joined the game to "even up" the number of players. However, he selected the best players for HIS team. It became a contest of the top 10 athletes against 11 scrubs, with my younger brother as their captain.

The most miraculous event in the history of PE class and the history of kickball unfolded! The kids on the scrub team—who usually did little more than trip over the ball—kicked base hits every time at the plate. Players who normally got hit in the face with the ball mysteriously made incredible diving catches as they achieved impossible outs.

On the Coach's superstar dream-team kickball squad, kids who normally kicked home runs couldn't kick their way out of a wet paper bag. Those who were superb athletes

Permission to be Tough
Raising Boys to be Rugged Gentlemen
Tim Austin

tripped and fell. Every player's eyes were on Coach as he kicked into a double play. Each kid became fully aware at the pivotal moment...when something snapped inside our record-setting coach's head.

In typical playground bully fashion, Coach reportedly went back to the plate and declared a "do-over." What students saw was a teacher exercising the privilege to change the rules any time he desired, right? As they pitched the ball, it was obvious to those on the field that REASON AND FAIRNESS were not part of the game that day; he summoned every volt of anger he could muster and directed it at the poor innocent kickball. With superhuman rage he kicked the ball further than any human being has ever kicked a kickball. It sailed over the outfield, across the street and into a neighboring apple orchard!

As the scrub outfielder loped to retrieve the ball from the fruit trees, the spectators were breathless. All eyes watched Coach direct high-voltage temper at the basemen. He arrogantly trotted around the bases as everyone viewed his vengeance—chest puffed out—head held high. The final shock came as he threw a forearm into the player on first base and knocked her 80-pound freshman body rolling in the dirt.

Pent-up anger pushed the uncontrolled coach forward. Second base was his undoing...the coach made the last and greatest mistake he would ever make as an employee of the school district—Coach hit the second baseman with his shoulder, knocked him to the ground, broke his glasses, ripped his shirt and embedded gravel under the skin on his arms. Stunned, 21 students watched a triumphant, albeit

Permission to be Tough
Raising Boys to be Rugged Gentlemen
Tim Austin

shameful, "role model" arrogantly trot around the bases. Coach did not notice how the baseman had picked himself up, broken glasses and all, and headed across the field for help and support.

The contemptuous coach didn't realize the second baseman's mom was the elementary school principal. I will just suffice it to say a mother's fury took on superhuman power. Coach saw her

> Poor choices by an adult put in charge of being a role model for students and athletes cannot end well.

heading his way with a baseball bat and realized she would bludgeon him if she caught him, so he made for a hasty exit. Not to overdramatize the event, but Coach—fueled by a combination of athleticism and fear—quickly hurdled the whirlpool, vaulted the equipment repair bench, grabbed his car keys in stride, and hit the back door of the locker room so hard it literally ripped off the hinges. He was never seen at school again.

There is one last message to this story and the examples that follow: Poor choices by an adult put in charge of being a role model for students and athletes cannot end well. Thankfully, I am happy to report, these students could see "right" wins. Life also has a way of providing justice! Coach never again graced the halls of the school; they terminated his employment. The athletes survived a very disturbing experience, and learned abuse and intimidation do not, in the long term, win.

Permission to be Tough
Raising Boys to be Rugged Gentlemen
Tim Austin

THE BEST AND THE WORST

Kids kind of get the luck of the draw with being under the tutelage of coaches. My brother's story is a prime example. While high school wrestling was one of the best experiences of my life, football and baseball were two of the worst, and it was mostly because of the coaching.

I recognized the coaches in my high school were the best or the worst; I also know this scenario plays out in schools all across the nation. But... you won't find a coach on this earth more respectful and tough than Coach Miller. Conversely, you can't find many worse coaches on earth than the coach previously discussed. Poor coaches play favorites, berate, or abuse their athletes, or treat kids with contempt and disrespect.

Imagine a kid who hits over .850 in the first 4 baseball games but sits the bench the rest of the season because a local business owner's son comes out late for baseball and is allowed the privilege of playing.

Imagine a player who sets a school rushing record his junior year sitting the bench his senior year because a school administrator's son wants to play running back.

Imagine a school official sitting behind the bench at basketball games and telling the coach who to play and what plays to run so that his son gets the most glory.

Imagine a school principal demanding that his son receives an award that another athlete has clearly won.

This is the stuff I saw in the world of high school sports when adults had their priorities all messed up. When greed,

Permission to be Tough
Raising Boys to be Rugged Gentlemen
Tim Austin

disrespect, and petty egos reign, kids are abused and defeated before they get to the field.

Just as a bad apple can spoil an entire bushel, so a bad administrator or coach can spoil an entire sports program. Fortunately, this kind of behavior is not the norm. But I mention it so that parents will beware of the rotten apples and know how to help their child respond, or how to take a stand for them.

CHAPTER 7
COACHES ROLE
TO INSPIRE AND CHALLENGE

———∞———

It's about the teaching, and what I always loved about coaching was the practices. Not the games, not the tournaments, not the alumni stuff. But teaching the players during practice was what coaching was all about for me.

~ John Wooden (1910-2010)
American Coach.

———∞———

SPORTS, FOR BOYS in particular, can be a great outlet for their energy and aggression. But more importantly, through sports, boys often learn respect for legitimate authority and rules in general. They also learn to follow the rules, listen to the coaches, respect opponents, and be thankful for the fans who came to watch their performance. Athletes often experience the value of hard work, effort, fair play. and the important lessons taught by winning and losing.

Permission to be Tough
Raising Boys to be Rugged Gentlemen
Tim Austin

In WINNING, boys learn to experience the thrill of success and the satisfaction of the reward for hard work.

In LOSING, boys experience the humility of falling short of their goals and the tenacity to come back and compete another day.

Both are valuable in shaping the character of a young man. To be sure, sports can be an incredible adventure or a horrible experience depending on the kid, the team, the coaching, and the behavior of the fans. As just one pertinent example, we have all witnessed the spectacle of the coach who tries to motivate and correct his young athletes using manipulation, threats, and coercion to get the kids to win at all costs. Young people often learn to hate sports and competition under these circumstances.

Personally, coaching taught me more than any single activity in my life—positively and negatively. As a young wrestler, some lessons I learned from Coach Miller, which extended way beyond high school and the wrestling mat include:

Courage,
tenacity,
fair play,
respecting rules,
respecting others,
strategy,
patience,
toughness, and
hard work.

Permission to be Tough
Raising Boys to be Rugged Gentlemen
Tim Austin

As a coach myself, I regularly learn things about:

people,
my wrestlers,
the sport,
the rules and
myself.

Each finds a way to carry on into my day-to-day life. You might recognize some that have also impacted your life, whether you were coaching a group of young boys, or trying to establish sportsman-like conduct in your son:

You may experience the need to drive an athlete to do something he doesn't want to do.

The art of great coaching inspires athletes to want to do what you want him to do.

Some boys will push themselves to exhaustion if you demonstrate that you believe in them.

It is possible for the human body to do far more, on far less food, than most people could imagine.

Your mind can convince your body to perform even when your body is crying and whining to stop.

Another great benefit that sports provides parents—if they dare to look objectively—is a realistic view of their kids. Unfortunately, few parents take advantage of that. Many parents act as though they think their child is an Olympic hopeful in every sport...no matter how unrealistic this may be.

Sports can answer a ton of questions parents have about their kids:

Permission to be Tough
Raising Boys to be Rugged Gentlemen
Tim Austin

Where do their strengths and weaknesses lie?
Where is their passion?
What are their interests?
What are they naturally good at doing?
With what do they naturally struggle?
How do their kids look at life?

An observant parent can help their child overcome perceived weaknesses while teaching the strategies children need to stress their actual strengths. It's all there wrapped up in a cool little package called "sports!"

There are several coaching philosophies, which are highly effective; you will find they work great. These range from "boot camp" tough to absurdly easy. To be honest, I am not a very "sweet" coach.

Discipline, hard work, toughness, grit, courage, and maximum effort and superior skill are characteristics I expect a child to develop. Because we draw on character-building skills like hard work, and because they've learned to respect each other.

I know many of my wrestlers win matches they shouldn't win—and often against much tougher and more skilled opponents. I fervently believe hard work, tenacity, fairness,

> I fervently believe how life works—hard work, tenacity, fairness, service, courage, and wisdom will triumph if a person is persistent in applying these qualities.

Permission to be Tough
Raising Boys to be Rugged Gentlemen
Tim Austin

service, courage, and wisdom will triumph if a person is persistent in applying these qualities.

In my humble opinion, to coach kids with respect is one of the most important activities a man can take part in if his passion is to impact our world profoundly. Coaching is the opportunity to influence young athletes in a manner few others can.

The situations of severe trials in coaching have taught me several concepts and ideas that may help you become a better and more respectful coach to your son. Take your time reading through them; make notes of those you could implement within your own life.

AUSTIN'S AXIOMS OF RESPECTFUL COACHING

CARE ONLY AS much as your young athlete cares. As a parent—or a coach—your frustration will be far less when you learn to care the same amount these young athletes care about the sport. We've all seen a well-meaning dad pushing his kid to be a professional ballplayer at the ripe old age of seven. It is likely each of us may have winced as a demanding, intense dad screamed and yelled at a kid who in his eyes just wasn't in the game. Find the level your kid needs. A few of the greatest things a father or coach can do for some kids are to:

Inspire them to care more about the game.
Encourage them to put forth more effort.
Challenge them to develop a good attitude.

NO SPORTS EVENT is worth destroying a kid over. There is no championship worth insulting, exasperating, berating, badgering, humiliating, frustrating or destroying your kid to

Permission to be Tough
Raising Boys to be Rugged Gentlemen
Tim Austin

win. The value of the human soul is infinitely more valuable than money, possessions, parental pride, or bragging rights. Destroying a kid's heart, mind and soul is monumentally disrespectful.

CHALLENGE, ENCOURAGE AND inspire your athletes. **Inspire** your athletes to care more, work harder, try new methods, think strategically, gain skills, act courageously, win graciously, and lose like a true sportsman. **Encourage** them in the tough times to develop better habits, keep their head in the game, and work more than their opponents. **Challenge** them to reach a higher level of performance, grow, change, and achieve more.

THE VALUE OF a child is far more than the ability to win a sporting contest. No matter what the age of the youthful athlete, each can only control certain elements of his game. He can control the amount of effort put forth, his energy, attitude, development of skills, and what someone learns from each loss and each victory. Beyond that, the opponent may have something to say about who wins or loses.

CREATE ESTABLISHED DISCIPLINE by setting standards and expectations, which are communicated clearly and consistently. It is unfair to a young athlete to expect him to perform a task for which you have not trained him. Expectations of behavior, sportsmanship, effort, growth, and attitude are important so that an athlete knows properly how to conduct himself. Each of these traits is foundational to all of life, not just the sport.

DEMONSTRATE YOUR BELIEF in athletes in your charge as a coach or father because this might be one of the most

Permission to be Tough
Raising Boys to be Rugged Gentlemen
Tim Austin

important things you can do for a kid, period. If you notice something grips a kid with doubt and fear about themselves and their world—go the extra mile to show you believe in them. When you genuinely give them a vision of what they can become, it increases the likelihood of building hope, incentive, and confidence.

WHEN IT IS within your capacity to orchestrate success for a child; embrace the frightened child whom you sense needs an adult to come alongside and show he can succeed. Does this require a little more effort on your part? Absolutely! Consider the child who has never caught a ball; maybe success for them is catching 10 throws in a row. What of another aspiring athlete who is trying to learn to ride a bike; you may help them feel successful even when they've learned to ride 50 ft. without falling. If you are the "athletic" father figure, you can probably relate to a boy who has never won a wrestling match; maybe you can give them the nudge to SCORE THAT FIRST TAKEDOWN.

ALTHOUGH IT SOUNDS counter-intuitive, it is equally important to orchestrate failure for each athlete. Just like winning, losing is a part of life. Learning to lose graciously in a sporting contest gives young athletes tools to deal with the myriad failures experienced later in life.

Learn the value of setting up a controlled situation wherein the athlete experiences failure; there is an enrichment in the opportunity to teach, correct, discipline, and affirm these life skills.

Permission to be Tough
Raising Boys to be Rugged Gentlemen
Tim Austin

Take advantage of the following suggestions as ways to empower your athlete or young son to live a higher standard.

REQUIRE RESPECTFUL BEHAVIOR by setting standards for athlete behavior and rules, such as respect your opponent; take part in fair play; and exhibit good sportsmanship.

SHARE WITH YOUNG athletes the traits that transfer into the grown-up world as a responsible citizen whereas, cheating or disrespecting your opponent can develop into far worse behavior when a rebellious young man is behind the wheel of a two-ton car.

SHOW THE VALUE of rules...kids learn that rules govern a sport. In fact, without rules and active enforcement of the rules, sports would not exist.

The better you know the rules of a particular game, the more you can strategically apply them to defeat your opponent. Rules govern a sport, but you can also use them to outmaneuver and outwit your opponent.

HELP ATHLETES OVERCOME their fears. For example, in the sport of wrestling, every wrestler must go out on the mat by himself to perform. It is natural to feel the intimidation, frustration, and emotional overwhelm, but by pushing himself to carry through, the wrestler can learn that fear is not fatal.

FEAR IS A temporary condition...overcome with courage. Send your athletes the message, "When wracked by fear, as

Permission to be Tough
Raising Boys to be Rugged Gentlemen
Tim Austin

a respectful coach I am more than willing to 'loan' you the courage until you develop your own."

TEACH YOUR SON to control his behavior, his attitude, and his tongue. It is beneficial for an athlete to display self-control in an aggressive situation. Bottom line...in sports, the aggressor usually wins. Although being aggressive on the field is an important attribute, the athlete must be able to know when to "turn it off."

As an out-of-control rebellious young man...you are a dangerous thing.

As a self-controlled humble young man...you become a person of character.

INSTRUCT YOUR ATHLETES respectfully. Treat them the way you would want to be treated. If you are in doubt about tactics to use, ask yourself...

"How would I want someone to treat me in this situation?"

> "When wracked by fear, as a respectful coach I am more than willing to 'loan' you the courage until you develop your own."

Few people want to experience disrespect; don't disregard your athletes. When they do something correctly, tell your athletes, "You got it right!" Cheer them on when they get it.

TELL YOUR ATHLETES the truth. If someone does a lousy job or displays minimal effort, don't lie to them, or say they performed well. He needs instruction and discipline to

Permission to be Tough
Raising Boys to be Rugged Gentlemen
Tim Austin

improve his skill. Praising a kid for half-hearted effort, lousy form, faulty execution, or failed strategy is tantamount to encouraging those behaviors. Be honest and praise him for something he is doing right—even just showing up can be a good thing. Praise him for that if you can't find anything else. But don't lie to the kid. It destroys your credibility because the truth is usually obvious.

> Teach a child to discover his own strengths; it will help develop self-awareness and confidence as an adult.

ACCURATELY ASSESS YOUR athlete's strengths and weaknesses; help him understand himself based on discernable actions and behaviors. Unfortunately, humans are adept at ignoring our own weaknesses and observing only our strengths. Teach a child to discover his own strengths; it will help develop self-awareness and confidence as an adult.

THEN, HELP THAT young man overcome his weaknesses. Unless an athlete sees and admits his skill or character flaws, he has little motivation to learn, improve, or grow and overcome that weakness. Honest self-examination is necessary for us to address the weaknesses in our lives, which need addressing and change. Kids learn hard work and tenacity when faced with their less than favorable skills or habits.

ALLOW ATHLETES TO be tough and aggressive—in a healthy manner. It generates toughness and tenacity between the

Permission to be Tough
Raising Boys to be Rugged Gentlemen
Tim Austin

ears of a fine athlete. A child who can push on in the face of pain or defeat can learn to persevere through real difficulties that life is certain to offer. Self-control and developing the ability to turn aggression on and off as is appropriate is especially important for kids to learn.

TEACH ATHLETES STRATEGIC thinking. By learning to outwit and out-hustle their opponent in sports, boys learn to think on their feet, both tactically and strategically, and to take advantage of opportunities. Success in life is full of situations, determined by tactical and strategic thinking.

HELP ATHLETES EXPERIENCE constant improvement. Unless pushed by external circumstances, most of us are content to remain as we are. To improve, an athlete must learn, grow, change, and adapt. Sports can be a primary vehicle for setting our youth on the path to learning and continual improvement over the balance of life.

BOYS NEED TO learn how to lose respectfully and win honorably. People should learn to be gracious no matter what circumstances they face in life. Somebody will defeat every athlete at some point—if he competes long enough. Learning to be gracious both in victory and defeat gives young athletes the tools to deal with both winning and losing later in life.

THINK ABOUT HOW watching and cheering can teach kids the overall strategic function of a sport. Life's lessons stay with us far longer when we learn by observing and doing; this is especially true in sports. What can you teach them as they observe the interaction between athletes, opponents, coaches, referees, and spectators? Help them better learn

Permission to be Tough
Raising Boys to be Rugged Gentlemen
Tim Austin

how the entire process of the contest works by engaging their actions and increasing their awareness.

DRILL, DRILL, DRILL. Practice is the art of putting kids in situations they will face on the sports field to give them tools for the game. We can break nearly every situation into small, understandable parts that can be simulated. Drills are a great method for giving kids the mental, physical, and emotional skills to deal with game situations. In reality, sports are a drill for actual life.

HAVE FUN! LET kids choose their preferred sport. You've seen the dad who lives for baseball and wants his son to follow in his footsteps, but the kid favors football. After a child has sampled different sports, what harm is there to respect his desire to participate in the sports for which he has the most interest? We can overwhelm kids as families rush from one sports venue to the next. Give the kid a break and give him some downtime.

APPROACH SPORTS AT the competition level your child needs or desires. We should not force a boy who wants to learn a sport at an entry-level league into an all-star professional development league. Kids develop at different rates physically, mentally, and emotionally. The best way to make a kid hate sports is to force him to compete at a level he is not ready to handle or a level he has already mastered.

TEACH ATHLETES TO compete honorably. A boy who learns to compete with respect and honor will have many of the tools he needs to live an honorable life. Teaching kids to cheat, bend the rules, or unfairly take advantage of an opponent who is not a worthy competitor is disrespectful. Need I

Permission to be Tough
Raising Boys to be Rugged Gentlemen
Tim Austin

mention the credibility you lose as a role model if you suggest they bend the rules or act outside the realm of personal integrity? Need I ask you the legacy such behavior would then leave for your son and the world in which you want him to grow?

A worthy competitor is one who is roughly your size, age, and skill level. For instance, if a professional boxer pummeled a novice, that behavior would be dishonorable. It is also not the mark of true achievement. With this thought in mind, seek to give awards to the true achievers. Kids know which players did a great job and whose skills, effort and abilities are lacking. It is dishonest to tell a kid he did a good job when he did a lousy job. It is dishonest to tell a kid he is the best when he isn't. You lose credibility for not telling the truth. Although we seem to live in a society that feels every child needs recognition, consider the merit of giving a couple awards per team for outstanding performance. I contend that to give every child in the program an award not only dilutes the value of the award given to the outstanding kid... it also discourages the drive toward peak performance inherent in most athletes.

CONSTANTLY AFFIRM GOOD behavior, effort, and attitude: We all need recognizing so tell kids what they are doing right— constantly. Remember, when you take the time to verbally praise someone it costs you nothing; alternatively, you will find they remember a well-timed and sincere compliment for a lifetime. Don't be stingy with your honest praise—and I reiterate, "Don't lie and tell an athlete that his effort and attitude are good if they stink."

Permission to be Tough
Raising Boys to be Rugged Gentlemen
Tim Austin

DEVELOP A POSITIVE culture. Coaches can grind on their kids and curse and scream to motivate them. Under that barrage of aggression, your athletes may win but I ask, "Is it worth destroying their humanity to do it?" Yelling positive instruction is far more effective than calling any athlete a derogatory name or to play non-productive head games with them.

Excellence is an easy word to speak but difficult to achieve.

If you think these philosophies are too wimpy or are simple excuses for being a mediocre coach to mediocre athletes, I would love to show each of these concepts in action while my kids kick the snot out of your team! Respectfully, notice that none of these concepts accepts disrespect, mediocrity, half-hearted effort, or lousy attitudes from kids.

If you think these philosophies are too hard and harsh, I'd invite you to talk to my sons and other athletes with whom I've coached who gladly worked harder when asked and inspired. I'd invite you to look at their skill level compared to their opponents and observe their unimpeachable attitudes and sportsmanship. Judge these coaching/parenting concepts by the fruit they produce. Add some of these concepts to your coaching methods and you will see the results.

The crux of valuing your athletes is this: If a coach sends a great kid out on the mat, a great kid comes off the mat at the end of the match, win or lose. If you send an arrogant little butthead out on the field or court, win, or lose, a little

Permission to be Tough
Raising Boys to be Rugged Gentlemen
Tim Austin

butthead comes back to the sidelines. The point is: what really matters is the value of the kid's attitude, heart, mind, body, soul, and character.

Winning is not everything. If you destroy a kid in the process of badgering him to win, what have you gained? If you break his will and destroy his love of the game, what have you gained? Whatever you think you gained, ask yourself, "Was it worth it?"

As a coach, I've learned to love coaching kids who have a great attitude, and who work hard to learn and grow. I don't care if this kind of kid loses every single match, if he continues in the right direction—armed with the right understanding of the correlation of sports and life, he will be a top-notch person someday. I far prefer a kid with a great attitude, who might lose every match, over the arrogant athletically gifted little knucklehead who screws around during practice, poisons the attitudes of other kids, and puts forth little effort... yet wins every match.

Can I speak to this from personal experience? You bet! I can't say I am overly proud to share that in junior high, I didn't win a single wrestling match. I can, however, speak differently about my senior year; I won the Colorado State Championship. What happened? My life was graced with a great coach who exemplified all the philosophies found above. Think of the impact you too can have on a child when you consider how his patience in instruction and his belief in me transformed a timid, puny seventh grade Tennessee transplant into a tough, confident, hardworking, young man.

Permission to be Tough
Raising Boys to be Rugged Gentlemen
Tim Austin

Non-Competitive Kids

Competition is not the only way for a kid to learn respect. Kids are all different; some are more passive and non-competitive by nature. Sports may or may not serve them well or help them grow and mature. A respectful man learns to respect people with differences and become comfortable to honor the path of life others have chosen. Does it not make sense then, that to manipulate a child to be something he is not able to be is, without a doubt, disrespectful for that child?

If the sports arena is not for your child, try music, art, auto mechanics, acting, design, woodworking, machine shop or a myriad of other activities to help him discover how to define his skills and talents, and through them... apply his strengths and overcome weaknesses.

Defending Softness

Inevitably some criticize the concept of becoming a Rugged Gentleman. Some people abhor fostering the toughness and courage that boys need to compete in this world. It is inevitable there will be criticism relative to the concept of ruggedness—in the proclamation that some boys will never be assertive; they are sweet and sensitive; they are kind and soft and they hate the competitiveness and aggressive behavior of others.

How would you respond to that kind of statement? My response is this: "The world can be a tough place where a person must compete to survive." Unless he plans to be a ward of the state for the rest of his life, he must compete. It is a natural part of life for everyone. Athletes, musicians,

Permission to be Tough
Raising Boys to be Rugged Gentlemen
Tim Austin

artists, actors, accountants, doctors, social workers, and even librarians compete at some level. Just because a person is kind, gentle, sensitive, and sweet doesn't mean he gets to avoid healthy competition in life. Something as necessary and ordinary as landing a job comes replete with competition amongst other applicants. If you buy a car or a home, you vie for your purchase against a myriad of other buyers in the market at the same time. You can't avoid competition in life, so accept reality and understand the dynamics of being competitive."

There is evidence all around us that—among other roles—the man's place in our culture is to be a protector and provider. What direction would our society turn if our young men grew to be too weak to protect their friends and families, or refused to protect those who are innocent? What detriment to our world if we raise men who shirk this one basic cultural role? It is our place in parenting and coaching to mentor the young man who is so naïve and inexperienced he won't be able to provide for himself and his family without help.

Some might say those that are weak earn shame and disgrace. In the past, it seemed the pressure applied by society was often enough to motivate a man to make the life transformation necessary to fulfill his duties to himself, his family, and his fellow citizens. That is no longer the case.

All around us we see the ill-effects on society brought about by men addicted, dependent, full of fear, full of rage, incarcerated, and living self-indulgent lifestyles. These men are often detached from their families and we see evidence they rarely care whether their kids have nurturing or

Permission to be Tough
Raising Boys to be Rugged Gentlemen
Tim Austin

training. Some males have lost the ability to care for and cherish the woman in their life or even feed and clothe their family members. The news is rife with the evidence where life's innocents struggle and suffer needlessly. We have raised a society of men no longer vested in being protectors. They may be rugged brutes, but they are not gentlemen in any sense of the word.

I am not advocating that all young men must become marines, weightlifters, cage fighters or drill instructors. I am, however, suggesting the need for young men to find their purpose in life, love the adventure, embrace courage, develop talents and skills, fight through pain, overcome failure, become protectors, provide for their families, serve their fellow man humbly and live lives of grace and character. I am also taking a stand for the boys who naturally excel at softer, more genteel interests prepare to become protectors and providers to the best of their abilities. I strongly promote that soft boys learn to become tough... and that tough boys learn to be genteel. Ultimately, I am fully in favor of a movement where we teach boys to understand when to be rugged and when to be gentle.

Yes! I get on a bandwagon about this topic. Rarely is the question asked, "Once you are dead and gone do you want your son to be a strong, healthy protector or would you prefer him to be weak, submissive and subservient to those who would take advantage of him?

CHAPTER 8
THE ATTITUDE OF A WINNER

You were born to win, but to be a winner, you must plan to win, prepare to win, and expect to win.

~ Zig Ziglar (1926-2012)
American Author, Motivational Speaker.

WHEN RAISING BOYS to be Rugged Gentlemen, harshness is a fine line that is seldom ok to cross. It is one thing to push a kid, expect a lot of him, assign him tough duties to fulfill, encourage him, help him, and walk shoulder to shoulder beside him in tough situations. But it is quite another to be harsh and unreasonable.

Harshness carries with it the connotation of cruelty and severity. True harshness can destroy a child's will. We must also be cognizant that what a boy in his level of youthful maturity may define as harsh may not be so at all. For instance, one of my sons might consider the request to turn off the television and do his homework to be the harshest and most unreasonable expectation ever. What we must

Permission to be Tough
Raising Boys to be Rugged Gentlemen
Tim Austin

focus on while raising a Rugged Gentleman is to nudge and push our boys to stop whining about life when it doesn't go their way—and to recognize the difference between harshness and healthy expectations.

The greatest coaches of all time in professional, college and high school sports are tough and courageous. They set remarkably high standards for their athletes. We often misunderstand their antics as harsh, but most of their athletes know the coach's methods will make each player the best individual player he can be to make the team the best it can be. A coaching method that one player perceives as reasonable tactics to draw the best out of a team, may be considered harsh and unreasonable to another player.

ATTITUDE OF A WINNER

For those of you young men who happen to be reading this book because you are looking to be the best you can be, the above paragraph reveals the formula. Do not view the coach's motives as anything but trying to make you the best. Because the minute you view him as harsh, you will not get any better. You will have shifted the responsibility from yourself, to put forth your best effort and energy, to hold the coach responsible for being an unreasonable "meanie."

Don't walk down that path! I otherwise know it as complaining, whining, and sniveling! The minute the coach becomes the enemy; as an athlete, you will find yourself traded, benched, or kicked off the team. Put yourself in the shoes of your coach... if he allows that kind of attitude

Permission to be Tough
Raising Boys to be Rugged Gentlemen
Tim Austin

around a team it will poison the attitudes of everyone on the team.

Most of the time the toughest coach gets the most out of his team. Toughness is not about belittling anyone, being rude or making threats. It is about loaning toughness, courage, and strength to the athletes. Mental toughness is what allows us to do our best. To be a champion, an athlete needs physical ability, mental toughness, and luck. The physical part is both natural and comes from hard work, eating right, working out properly, getting the proper amount of sleep and maybe even making your body do what it does not want to do. Luck is the wild card in any game: weather conditions, injuries, accidents, the opponent, or mishaps can determine success. The real athletes win and lose games...in their minds. The crux is mental. If you think you can't, you are correct—you won't. If you think you can, you have a shot at succeeding.

"Baseball is 90% mental—the other half is physical."

~Yogi Berra (1925-2015)
American professional baseball catcher.

Great coaches are tough, but they display the toughness that has success in sight at all times. It is not a roughness for

the sake of cruelty. It is courage and strength for the sake of becoming the best. It is a resolve for the sake of leading young men to do more than they ever imagined possible. It

Permission to be Tough
Raising Boys to be Rugged Gentlemen
Tim Austin

is giving athletes a vision much bigger and beyond themselves. If a coach is building men, his toughness is understandable and typically justified. However, if a coach is just competing to win at all costs regardless of the athletes, his toughness will probably be cruel and unjustified.

A Rugged Gentleman achieves status by transcending the whining and complaining common among average men. The danger of whining and complaining is that it is the attitude that generates sniveling words and an attitude of a quitter and a blamer or victim. The whiners and complainers are looking for an excuse to manipulate, control, give up, slack off, or quit. A wise parent doesn't put up with this kind of attitude in kids because a little wave of whining in a kid will turn into an angry tempest of blame and excuses in adulthood.

Be careful to avoid cursing your kid by allowing him to get away with a victim attitude. Be careful letting a kid quit mid-season because the going gets tough. Excuse making creates a modus operandi for the rest of his life. Beware of allowing a kid to blame others for his failure. The fact is that if a kid prepares himself better, learns what he is taught better than his opponent, puts forth more effort, learns better strategy, and prepares himself physically he will have a much better chance of being victorious.

CHAPTER 9
THE IDEAL SCHOOL FOR BOYS

*The principal goal of education in the schools should
be creating men and women who are capable of
doing new things, not simply repeating what other
generations have done.*

~ Jean Piaget (1896-1980)
Swiss Psychologist.

BROCK COULDN'T WAIT to get to school. He was starting his
freshman year at a brand-new high school. Normally,
freshmen dread the thought of being the bottom man on the
totem pole. Hazing, intimidation, and manipulation are the
norms for school life. But this school was different, vastly
different. A local businessman had figured out a way to
educate boys for less money but give them relevant classes
in a fun learning environment.

Every single class at the new school included math,
reading, writing, science, and history. Brock didn't like
writing all that much, but he had heard so much about the

Permission to be Tough
Raising Boys to be Rugged Gentlemen
Tim Austin

new school he wanted to give it a shot. A little writing would be bearable if everything else he had heard about the school was true.

As Brock rode his bike through the entrance gate, he could see the buildings at the end of the tree-lined road. As he pedaled up to the huge four-story cut stone building his eyes immediately made their way up the enormous bell tower with the huge clock mounted in the face. Following his gaze all the way back down to the ground he saw a sign that read, "Choose any Class". Underneath was a list of classes with an arrow pointing left or right toward the buildings in which the classes were meeting. The list included Wood Shop, Stables, Machine Shop, Automotive Shop, Shooting Range, Ropes Course, Orchard, Music, Sports Complex, Moto-X, Library, Computer Lab, Writing Lab, Snack Shack, Ball Room, Marina, Oration & Debate, Golf Course, Tennis Courts, Science Lab, and Equipment Barn.

This was more than a little confusing. Where should he go? Finally, Brock made his way to the stable area to see what it was all about. He pedaled around the main building and headed toward the barn and horse stables. He parked his bicycle in the bike rack outside the barn door and stepped into the loading alley of the barn. A kind voice met him from the office beside the entrance. "Care for a morning ride?" Startled, Brock stepped toward the open office door and said, "Excuse me?" Mr. Overton stepped from his office with his hand extended, "I'm Mr. Overton, the stable director. I was getting ready to saddle my horse and go for a ride. Care to saddle up and join me?"

Permission to be Tough
Raising Boys to be Rugged Gentlemen
Tim Austin

"Uh, no, sir. I mean, yes sir," Brock stammered as this stranger motioned toward the stables and walked toward the horses.

Mr. Overton showed an amazed Brock how to bridle a horse and remove a halter from underneath the headstall. He explained all the tack, showed Brock how to check the horse's shoes without getting kicked, curry comb his withers, cut cockleburs from his mane, check for saddle sores, and saddle the horse. Mr. Overton saddled his horse and off they rode around the 850-acre campus through the beautiful mowed lawns and huge hardwood trees.

They rode by the Moto-X dirt track where boys were running a test heat to get accustomed to the jumps and water hazards. The football field and track were the busiest spots with at least 50 boys practicing football and a dozen more runners loafing through a few warm-up laps. As they rode through the middle of the ropes course, an instructor had to spend a great deal of one-on-one time with his one student to make sure he got it right; a fall from one of the 40-foot towers could be fatal.

Riding along the firing line of the shooting range made both horses edgy and skittish but the range master called "cold" to give time to pass before one of the horses spooked. Actually, the boys on the firing line opened their weapons and carefully laid them down to go down range and mount new targets, anyway. Mr. Overton and Brock really weren't much of a disruption for the small arms rimfire class. An hour later they pulled up to the hitching rail outside the stable. Mr. Overton dismounted and motioned for Brock to do the same. They removed the saddles and tack and

Permission to be Tough
Raising Boys to be Rugged Gentlemen
Tim Austin

brushed the horses. They turned both horses into a metal corral shaded by a huge maple tree. The horses would spend the day outside today.

Brock asked Mr. Overton where he should go for class. Mr. Overton chuckled and walked into his office and returned with a small booklet.

"Here is your school outline. You must first complete a Basic class in 25 disciplines in each lab or shop. That normally takes a couple of years. After that, you get to choose 4 disciplines you want to specialize in. That is when you work one-on-one with every instructor learning how to teach the basics. You spend your last two years teaching the Basics classes and mentoring the younger boys. They expect the boys you mentor to know as much as you know by the end of each Basics class. You will write a report each day and turn it into your mentor. And you'd better make sure you learn to write well, because at the end of our 4 years here you will have an entire manual, in your own handwriting, on how to operate, shoot, repair, maintain, play and cultivate everything on the campus." Mr. Overton paused.

"Any questions?"

"Uh, no, uh, yea, where do I start?" Brock asked.

"Anywhere you want," Mr. Overton replied.

Puzzled, Brock's eyes lit up, "Anywhere?"

"Anywhere you want, son."

Brock's education dream…. he realized; this school would be tough, but he would learn relevant skills and life

Permission to be Tough
Raising Boys to be Rugged Gentlemen
Tim Austin

lessons. Truly, this was only his dream; nothing like it actually exists.

SCHOOL DAZE

SOMEWHERE ALONG THE way, our schools evolved into a system that throws hundreds of hormone-crazed kids into the same building so that overworked unionized teachers can try to teach them information that is somewhat irrelevant to their lives. A school is a place where boys are expected to sit in nice rows, keep their hands to themselves, keep their mouths shut, sit still, and do their "nice" work quietly... at the urging of a well-meaning female teacher who defines what "nice work" looks like. Nice work to most teachers is irrelevant busy work for most boys. But that work, mandated by the politicians, school administrators, and teachers causes boredom and frustration felt by many boys, and is a set-up for hyperactive behavior and mischief by any normal kid. No wonder our school officials insist on drugging the boys to settle them down enough so they can sit and do their pretty work. This sounds like "Boy-Hell."

Females developed our current school system—for girls. I know, I know, most of you bristle at that suggestion. Some of you can even point to your feminized son who loves school because he likes to sit still and engage in pretty work. You can poll boys... acclimated in the world of girls, and they will tell how much they love sitting in nice rows and doing nice work. But give real boys an actual alternative method of learning and you will see their eyes light up.

Permission to be Tough
Raising Boys to be Rugged Gentlemen
Tim Austin

If you are anything like me, you are probably doing a risk analysis in your head and mentally calculating the cost of liability insurance for a school that boys would enjoy. You are probably trying to figure out how to manage a school with guns, horses, motorcycles, loud music, food, tools, engines, boxing gloves, wrestling mats, writing labs, and experimentation stations. You are probably envisioning a 10-story office building across the street from the ideal boys' school full of liability lawyers. As in real life, just the thought of lawyers stifles even the fantasy of a relevant and instructive school design, let alone setting it up.

In reality, our current education system is all lawyers will allow. In our school systems today are many excellent teachers who could turn learning into a profound activity for kids but for a government monopolistic system, labor unions, and the laws that govern the education system. But sadly, a big percentage of our teachers go through the motions because they came into teaching with idealism and energy but have had all that wrung out by unreasonable administrators, angry parents, apathetic kids and a culture that does not embrace innovation and change. Because of the lack of leadership in school administrations, great teachers learn to play the game and get through the day. The students are the ones short-changed.

STACKED DECK

The deck is stacked against many boys. Because of over-protective or over-stressed moms, distant or absent dads, schools designed for girls, addictions and the lack of healthy stimuli to capture a boy's imagination and interest, it is a

Permission to be Tough
Raising Boys to be Rugged Gentlemen
Tim Austin

wonder any boys ever reach adulthood with a healthy sense of who they are. It is no wonder schools don't experience more shootings and violence. This culture of neglect and abandonment of boys is coming home to roost as we see more school shootings, road rage, street racing, theft, teen pregnancy, and vandalism in many US cities.

The bleakness of the situation would depress any boy but for the bright spots in his life that pull him back from the brink. Luckily, boys get to take part in sports, outdoor activities, watch healthy movies and read good books. Sometimes, they get to learn from the few dedicated teachers still trying their best to teach, demanding coaches who call them to a higher standard, and, fortunately, most times, loving parents who take seriously their duty to raise healthy respectful kids. And a big pat on the back goes to the kids, surrounded by the seedy ugly side of life, who staunchly refuse to take part in activities that bring them down or cheapen their lives. Those young men are the ones I am looking to hire to run my business.

Permission to be Tough
Raising Boys to be Rugged Gentlemen
Tim Austin

CHAPTER 10
BOY ON A LEASH

―――――――∽∾――――――――

*Older people sit down and ask, "What is it?'" but the
boy asks, "What can I do with it?"*

~ Steve Jobs (1955-2011)
American Businessman.

―――――――∽∾――――――――

AGAINST POPULAR BELIEF, parenting is not about controlling
and manipulating kids. All my life I have heard parents make
comments pertaining to controlling their kids. Mostly, those
comments came from frustrated parents who have set
themselves up for failure and frustration by trying
desperately to control their offspring.

It is hard to control boys! It frustrates many parents,
who try to control their kids, but fail. It is possible to lead,
convince, persuade, urge, induce, reason with, beg, direct,
pull, show, plead with, press, and ask. But boys have a
natural resistance to being forced to do anything. You may
force him to comply for a while, but you will not force or
control a boy for long. And to do so may be folly and

Permission to be Tough
Raising Boys to be Rugged Gentlemen
Tim Austin

destructive. Boys, like their dads, want to be asked and convinced to act on their own free will, not forced, coerced, or manipulated. It is a trait of human nature.

Don't get caught up in the exceptions. If a child runs in the street, sure, they must force him to the sidewalk for his own safety. When danger is imminent, a child might experience the force of a parent, coach, etc. If a child is raising a bottle of poison, we must force him to surrender the harmful substance. To reckon and reason with a child in such situations is foolish. Ultimately, the child needs sufficient knowledge that running into the street or drinking poison is harmful. Someone must give him the understanding that a car might hit him, or the poison will make him sick to the point of death. But otherwise convincing a boy to act is far more effective than forcing him.

Eventually, it is natural for the child to discover and develop the wisdom to discern for himself and control his own behavior. Until a child has the knowledge of danger, we must impress upon them the understanding of risk and the wisdom to practice self-control to regulate his own behavior to comply with rules and directives. So, after a child gains the knowledge, understanding, and wisdom to make rational decisions, given the respect of convincing, persuading and asking for compliance stacks higher than force. Force brings up one reaction from men: resistance.

We should treat children with respect and dignity at all times. Beating a child is horribly disrespectful. Ripping apart a child's heart with cutting words and cruel comments is detestable. Starving a child's soul by depriving him of affection, warmth, and kindness is merciless. Anyone who

Permission to be Tough
Raising Boys to be Rugged Gentlemen
Tim Austin

practices these "parenting" techniques forgets how much they would hate to have these tactics used on them. In practicing disrespectful behavior toward their kids—we have only the results of rebellion and defiance.

Still, refusing to discipline a defiant, rebellious child is also neglectful and ultimately does him harm. So how should you discipline a child? The answer is, with respect and honor. Make the consequences of his original choice so unpleasant that he sees your way of doing things and complies with your wishes. If your child refuses to eat his vegetables, don't feed him ice cream or cookies for dessert until he finishes the veggies. If he still refuses, refrigerate his vegetables, and serve them for breakfast and don't feed him anything else until he eats them. Teach him to hold his nose and eat so he doesn't taste them. Help him understand that if he eats the vegetables with a bite of meat, he won't dislike the taste as much. Whatever it takes, work through the problem and help him resolve the issue without you giving in. Refusing to eat veggies is not worthy of spanking but is worthy of a bit of persuasion.

Does this mean a parent must match wits and argue with their child? Absolutely not! To match wits with a child is foolish. Parental authority is a power given to parents because they are parents. For a child to argue with an adult is horribly disrespectful. For a parent to perpetuate the argument with the child is foolish. As a parent, you have the authority to say "no" and mean "no". And for a child to ask disrespectfully, "why", as if the parent owes him an answer, is beyond the pale. Any parent who puts up with rude behavior teaches their child to be arrogant and disrespectful.

Permission to be Tough
Raising Boys to be Rugged Gentlemen
Tim Austin

Anytime you attempt to force a rational adult to do something, you are being disrespectful toward him, showing contempt for his free will and disregarding his sovereignty as a human being. To be clear, "force" is the act of compelling, coercing, controlling, making, extorting, taking, or imposing. Anytime you disregard the reasonable free choice of another adult you are not respecting his sovereignty as a person.

If you practice manipulation, coercion, and force on family members, coworkers, or neighbors, I challenge you to grow up and respect people. If your parenting style includes these tactics, I challenge you to consider alternatives for the sake of the precious lives of your kids. Force is the practice of brutal dictators, despots, and tyrants. There is a better way to treat kids and loved ones. Ask yourself; "would I like the same treatment I dish out to my spouse, my kids, my family members, my coworkers or my fellow man?" If not, it is time to look deep inside and make a major change in attitude and behavior.

CHAPTER 11
COPING IN A COMPLICATED WORLD

Learn something from everyone you meet.

~ Abraham Lincoln (1809-1865)
American statesman and lawyer who served as the 16th
President of the United States.

BEFORE THE INDUSTRIAL Revolution, most people in the world grew up in an agrarian society. Older members of the extended family taught the younger members. They disciplined and trained the children, passing on skills and experience learned from generations before. We invited boys into the world of "men" by working, playing, helping, and learning alongside their dads, uncles, grandfathers, and cousins. In these extended families, the patriarch handed off management of family land and wealth after his prime. At that point, the younger men took control and managed the family assets so that the patriarch could still help them learn before he retired to take comfort in his old age.

Permission to be Tough
Raising Boys to be Rugged Gentlemen
Tim Austin

Under this model, the younger men managed the assets in the prime of their life. With the extended family living in proximity, training, discipline, and experience helped these young men handle the task. Young men had the ability to manage well by the time parents passed the family land and wealth to them.

Before the Industrial Revolution, extended families lived together in the same house or in the same village. The citizens of the village helped raise the children. Today, kids move away from home at 18 and rarely live close to their extended family, so we have little support and training from our elders.

Today, when an 18-year-old "man" leaves his home, he often substantially cuts his ties and uproots himself. Much of what he learns is done with no extended family around to continue to teach him. He depends on his peers for learning that information, and we all know the quality and value of the knowledge of a herd of 18-year-old males.

The notion of the village assisting in child rearing was a welcome reality a few generations ago. It was a proper model and a necessary framework for raising kids in that era. Today having disrespectful people helping me raise my kids isn't as charming. Frankly, I don't want my kids learning what rude, disrespectful people have to teach them. To be sure, there are some wonderful people in our society, but I do not want to risk today's "village" idiots, child molesters, drug addicts, emotional basket cases, rebellious self-worshipers, and arrogant social engineers raising my kids. I am sure the feeling is mutual.

Permission to be Tough
Raising Boys to be Rugged Gentlemen
Tim Austin

The extended-family model provides a more long-term view of how to raise children and a more interdependent model for family. The contrast between that model and the change in family structure today sheds light on the discord and disharmony in our culture. It also gives us hints about the thinking that is fracturing our culture. The family unit has historically been the building block of our culture. In our present culture, it is often a fractured structure... splintered and reflected in a crumbling society.

Think of the complications for a kid if his parents didn't teach him much about respect and getting along in the world. Think of the tragedy if his parents treated him so badly that he can't or doesn't want to continue a relationship with them. If you throw an inexperienced, immature, and bewildered young man into the world, he suffers trying to figure out life.

COMPLICATED WORLD

The world is far more complicated than it was just 30 years ago. In the past, people went to work, paid their bills, went to school, raised their kids, and enjoyed a hobby or two. Today, much more is required of people to get along. Take the example of buying a house. Thirty years ago, you filled out a simple contract and a credit application. When your loan was approved, the escrow closing was simple, and you moved in and lived. To purchase a house today, you fill out a six-page contract and a four-page credit application in triplicate. Get a home inspection, a mold certification, radon certification, lead paint inspection, furnace certification, roof certification, tax district certification, easement certification,

Permission to be Tough
Raising Boys to be Rugged Gentlemen
Tim Austin

energy code certification, homeowner's association covenants, real estate tax certificate, wastewater drainage fee schedule, school district fee notification, hazard insurance certificate, fire district assessment, property tax notification, aluminum wiring certification, asbestos certification, an expansive soil notification, an appraisal, utility applications, telephone application, trash service application, lawn refuse dump permit, and the list goes on and on for every different county in the U.S. Nobody can keep up with it all and know all that is necessary to buy a house.

During your two-hour real estate closing, each party has to sign roughly 27 different documents and are legally bound to know what each document means and the ramifications of signing each one. No wonder kids get so frustrated when they realize the complications, we have piled on them. And this is only for the small part of life involved in purchasing a house. Think of all the myriad of complications involved in every other area of life. Is it any wonder so many 20-something kids move back in with mom and dad?

CHAPTER 12
DETHRONING THE LITTLE PRINCE

*No horse gets anywhere until he is harnessed. No
stream or gas drives anything until it is confined. No
Niagara is ever turned into light and power until it
is tunneled. No life ever grows great until it is
focused, dedicated, and disciplined.*

~ Harry Emerson Fosdick (1878-1969)
American Clergyman.

IN FAMILY STRUCTURE, fewer adults today will establish the
pecking order with children or enforce respect for that
hierarchy. Thus parents, teachers, and youth leaders
experience frustration when kids don't respect authority. A
heavy-handed, mean-spirited approach is unnecessary to
teach this respect. However, when warranted they provide
painful consequences if a kid's rebellious heart requires it.

Children are happy to learn respect and honor when
treated with the same respect and honor we ask of them.

Permission to be Tough
Raising Boys to be Rugged Gentlemen
Tim Austin

Children learn respect, submission, and leadership when they see it modeled by respectful adults. Children learn to self-regulate their behavior when they see respectful adults apply self-control to their own lives. Children learn moderation, common sense, and wisdom when they see adults practicing these virtues.

RAISING BOYS AND THE HIERARCHY OF AUTHORITY

When a boy does not submit to the hierarchy of authority around him as he grows up, he often becomes disrespectful, ungrateful, rebellious, and spoiled. If he hasn't been taught, and if he doesn't see it modeled, he may never understand legitimate authority. This is one reason many young people today do not understand how to relate to other people respectfully. This is one reason many young people don't understand or respect their place in life, and their place in society. Boys must learn or be convinced to accept the concepts of hierarchy and respect that govern all men. To allow a boy to live as if he is the top dog in every arena of life is neglectful and crippling. His arrogant attitude will bring rejection and isolation as adults fail to accept his lofty opinion of himself.

In the process of raising boys, it is wise to foster a sense of urgency, need, want, and hunger to motivate them to learn, grow, and become wise adults. The struggle is necessary for young men. Just as a butterfly must struggle out of the cocoon or his wings won't work, so a young man must struggle to grow and understand the world around him. To hand a young man everything he wants is to spoil him and destroy his incentive.

96

Permission to be Tough
Raising Boys to be Rugged Gentlemen
Tim Austin

Releasing a mature, respectful young man into the world is an exciting event. He gets to go out and apply himself to see how he "measures up" to the world, to other men, to leaders of his industry, and to everyone he encounters.

Conversely, releasing a rebellious, addicted butthead into society is an affront and an insult to everyone he comes in contact with. It is a sorrowful event that highlights the attitude of rebellion by the kid or failure to teach properly and discipline by the parents.

When parents or teachers tolerate children who bully, harm, or tear down others, they are teaching kids that abuse is acceptable. When men teach their boys to fight to defend themselves, their families, the weak, and the innocent they release to the world a young man who is tough and able to tackle the problems life throws at him. In the process of learning toughness, the boy must learn self-control and when to turn on the aggression and when to turn it off.

Life experiences that require kids to learn respect are great ways for young men to learn to submit to the hierarchy of authority and respect. Good examples include military organizations, cotillion, etiquette, grooming in business, sports under a respectful coach, golf, martial arts, and farming.

Permission to be Tough
Raising Boys to be Rugged Gentlemen
Tim Austin

"The next best thing to being wise oneself is to live in a circle of those who are."

~ CS Lewis (1898-1963)
British writer and lay theologian.

Boys, especially, need to experience respect in every form. Another aspect of respect that is subtler but particularly important is body language and physical demonstrations of honor. Boys must learn that it is rude to take a seat at the head of the table without first being asked to do so. When they learn respect for podiums, stages, platforms, and elevated places they will properly respect the position of those who are up on the elevated places. Boys who understand the idea of purposely positioning themselves in lower places relative to older, respectful people will gain respect and honor because of their attitude and behavior. We will respect boys who learn to avoid positioning themselves to "stand over" men who are seated. When a boy stands and shakes the hand of a respectful man during an introduction, he gains respect and honor for his wise behavior. Proper body position can project respect while improper body position can project disrespect.

Permission to be Tough
Raising Boys to be Rugged Gentlemen
Tim Austin

"You can preach a better sermon with your life than with your lips."

~ Oliver Goldsmith (1728-1774)
Irish novelist, playwright, and poet.

STEERING A CHILD

So, what is the "right" road for a child? An adult generally possesses a more mature view of life and the world than a child owns. To allow a child to "guide" himself is foolish and cruel. Parents who guide and direct a child in their thoughts and behaviors give him a huge advantage in life. Teaching him Classic Respect gives a boy a framework by which to live his life and self-regulate his behavior.

ARGUING WITH A CHILD

It is foolish to argue with a child. In fact, to argue with anyone who doesn't use good judgment and good sense is to participate in a fool's game. You will argue from a warped frame of reference. Such an argument provides no possible victory for you. Allowing a child to argue teaches him he is a worthy opponent to match wits with you. To argue with a child is to allow him to frame the debate and draw you in. Although arguing with a child is foolish, answering respectful questions will help him adopt a healthy frame of reference. Asking "why" questions are often the child's attempts to find a reason to self-regulate his behavior. They

Permission to be Tough
Raising Boys to be Rugged Gentlemen
Tim Austin

should treat the disrespectful "why" as defiance and rebellion because that is the attitude it signifies.

What is the difference between legitimate and defiant "why" questions? If a child is seeking knowledge, understanding, and wisdom, to avoid answering his "why" is disrespectful to him. If a child is seeking to stall, change the subject, be argumentative or manipulate the situation, to answer his "why" is playing into his mental chess game of rebellion.

"Never argue with a fool in his foolishness."

~ Proverbs

Children are typically not equal to adults in reasoning and communication skills. To treat a child as a peer and not enforce the hierarchy of respect is to allow him to elevate his own position in his own mind. Arrogance is the natural result of thinking more highly of oneself than one ought to think.

In the late 1980s, a movement emerged in education that sought to "empower" children. Who in their right mind thought up the idea to empower immature, inexperienced little people? Fortunate for all involved, the movement has subsided somewhat, but through it all many kids learned to flex their verbal muscles in disrespect to their parents.

Permission to be Tough
Raising Boys to be Rugged Gentlemen
Tim Austin

RESPECTFUL PARENTING

Respectful parenting requires patience and wisdom. Kids who can see a wide variety of life experiences typically grow up to be more courageous, well-rounded, and wise. When kids have the freedom to fail and grow without harsh criticism or unrealistic expectations, they are more confident and gracious. The respectful parent consistently offers their children a vision and a model to imitate. Kids may not know who they are until an adult tells them and shows them what they can do and be in life.

"If we take the accepted definition of bravery as a quality which knows no fear, I have never seen a brave man. All men are frightened. The more intelligent they are, the more they are frightened. The courageous man is the man who forces himself, in spite of his fear, to carry on."

~ General George Patton (1885-1945)
American Soldier.

WELL-ROUNDED

To truly be well-rounded, parents might teach a boy both how to dig ditches and dance with the daughter of a king. They would teach him to cook his own meals and eat exotic foods he might otherwise find repulsive. He might learn to build a house or tear down an engine. He might have to learn

Permission to be Tough
Raising Boys to be Rugged Gentlemen
Tim Austin

to manage a business and manage his emotions. All boys need to have common sense and a great sense of humor.

A boy is much more confident when he learns to converse on a wide range of subjects. A working knowledge of everything from astrophysics to microbiology, music to real estate, boats to weapons, aviation to geology, psychology to satire, religion to politics, comics to classics, and everything in between makes for a well-rounded young man. Knowledge and understanding gleaned from one topic often lead to learning in other areas. Focusing only on one topic, however, often leads to arrogance and a narrow view of the world while broad knowledge of a variety of topics makes a young man humble.

Our society often rewards specialists over generalists. By definition, a specialist knows a great deal about one subject. This frequently leads to arrogance and a know-it-all attitude. Men with a wide range of experience and knowledge have greater common sense and a humble attitude. Having a wide range of general knowledge allows one to realize how little he really knows about the world. This leads a respectful man to realize just how much wisdom exists in this world, how little of it he has, and how much wisdom is available for the taking if you will work to get it.

"You must be the change you wish to see in the world."

~ Mahatma Gandhi (1869-1948)
Indian Leader.

CHAPTER 13
BORROWED COURAGE

Courage is being scared to death... and saddling up anyway.

~ John Wayne (1907-1979)
Actor.

AS BOYS, WE all encountered situations where we were afraid and felt abandoned or alone. If you had a great dad who sensed your thoughts and your plight, you may have received support and help through those tough situations. However, from all the men I have talked with, if you received that help and support you would be one of a mere handful of boys who did.

In tough times, one of the deepest longings in the heart of a young boy is to have a strong man put a warm arm of understanding around his shoulders and assure him. Mind you, boys don't need a man to rescue them. Boys need a man to walk alongside. When boys experience the pain of disappointment, the embarrassment of failure, the agony of

Permission to be Tough
Raising Boys to be Rugged Gentlemen
Tim Austin

defeat or suffer the heavy burden of separation and loss, they don't NEED someone or something to take the pain away. Although that is what we all want, it is not what we NEED. What we need is someone to walk alongside us through the grueling ordeal.

When parents try to take the pain away by ensuring that their child doesn't suffer the consequences of their own stupidity, the kid will never learn. He will continue to repeat the bad behavior and make the same stupid choices until he faces the pain of the painful consequences or punishment for his mistakes. Boys don't need someone to shield them from the pain of their bad behavior; they need someone to walk beside them, shoulder to shoulder, as they go through it.

BORROW AND LOAN: PAYING IT FORWARD

I refer to the previous scenario as loaning and borrowing courage and support. Even in my mid-forties, if I am being impatient with someone, I need a RUGGED GENTLEMAN nearby who will loan me his patience and understanding, and to call me on my bad behavior so I will improve. If I am doing something foolish, I need someone to loan me their wisdom and humbly walk with me through the situation.

Eventually, I won't need to borrow the wisdom, I will have my own to loan to others. We have talked about courage, patience, and wisdom. Some other things loaned and borrowed between men include knowledge, understanding, good attitude, toughness, kindness, skill, humor, honesty, persistence, good character, positive outlook, righteous behavior, self-control, a tender nature, a

Permission to be Tough
Raising Boys to be Rugged Gentlemen
Tim Austin

healthy world view, powerful self-image, good habits, and faith.

The first reason I refer to this concept as borrowing is because after a period of borrowing, eventually you won't need the help because you will have developed that character trait in yourself from the seed you borrowed from others.

Second, in years to come, you will loan to others what you borrowed years before. Similar to the concept of PAY IT FORWARD, you borrow from people and don't pay them back because you will loan to others later without expectation of payback.

Third, character traits are not things purchased and sold; they are far more precious than money.

And finally, borrowing and lending bring with them the expectation of a long-term commitment between two parties for a much longer-term relationship than a single transaction connotes.

Permission to be Tough
Raising Boys to be Rugged Gentlemen
Tim Austin

CHAPTER 14
HOW TO HANDLE BOYS TESTING LIMITS

In every real man a child is hidden that wants to play.

~ Friedrich Nietzsche (1844-1900)
German Philosopher

IN TRIBAL CULTURES around the globe, rituals are often performed when a boy passes from the tender gentleness of his mom's care to the rugged toughness of his dad's world. Tribal leaders conduct these rites of passage when a boy reaches 10—14 years of age. Moms step aside. They play a diminishing role in the boy's life as he learns to be a man.

In some cultures, these rites of passage may look like a kidnapping as they take the boy from the comfort of his mom's house to the communal home of the men. In other cultures, it may look like a party complete with pomp and circumstance. Other cultural rites of passage may include painful rituals, recitation of ancient wisdom or a solitary journey and adventure into the wild. But no matter the

Permission to be Tough
Raising Boys to be Rugged Gentlemen
Tim Austin

details, many cultures have a set time or event that separates a boy from his soft childhood.

These ceremonies signal to everyone that the boy has passed from boyhood to the start of manhood. His life changes because of this passage into the man's world. He now associates more with boys and men. His new status allows him to hunt, gather food, or leave home to seek work as he increasingly gains independence from his mother's nurturing.

CULTURAL INDIFFERENCE

Sadly, as a whole, our culture lacks such rituals and events. Aside from occasional religious ceremonies, boys do not have an event that marks their passage from boyhood to manhood. Therefore, a boy may be a boy forever. Or he may join his friends and create his own rite of passage rituals (sometimes involving hazardous or illegal behaviors) or he may declare his independence and pretend to be a man far before he is ready.

What is worse, our society has established many roadblocks and diversions to passaging a boy into manhood. It might be more accurate to say we provide boys with too many leisure activities, opportunities to be lazy, playthings to enable their immaturity and irresponsibility. Our society is full of 30 and 40-year-old TEENAGERS because life seems to have not afforded them encouragement or expectations to become men.

Some dads abandon their sons altogether. Some subcultures of our society experience fathers are rarely

Permission to be Tough
Raising Boys to be Rugged Gentlemen
Tim Austin

present or involved in the boy's life at all. In some communities, if the man is around, he is irresponsible, violent and crime prone as he models horrible behavior for the boys who are watching. In these situations, the dad only passes along bad attitudes, entitlement mentality, slothful behavior, anger, and resentment.

Still, too many youths in our culture raise themselves with parents who are absent due to work. Sometimes they only have input from other kids. Street gangs are a classic example. There is nothing good that can come of a bunch of contemptuous punks teaching younger arrogant punks how to live. That is a formula for a disaster which is the best term to describe many young men in our culture: DISASTERS.

> Our society is full of 30 and 40-year-old TEENAGERS because life seems to have not afforded them encouragement or expectations to. become men.

Another tragedy of wasted minds is manifested when boys sit in front of a TV playing video games every day after school, during school vacations and every weekend...to boot. Violent video games and movies are sometimes the primary home influence for young lads. At school, most teachers are females who may or may not understand and appreciate the energy and behavior of normal boys. And who can blame her for feeling frustration as she tries to teach a room full of

Permission to be Tough
Raising Boys to be Rugged Gentlemen
Tim Austin

hyperactivity? Tough teachers have an influence, yet the dominant influence at school is other kids. And we all know how much healthy information a 14-year-old boy can impart to his friends. Some boys have little or no chance to associate with a strong healthy male who can model healthy behavior.

RECIPE FOR DISASTER

Ingredients: Start by acknowledging the increasing number of predators of our society who prey on boys for their sick, demented molestation fantasies. Throw in the vicious divorces where parents are so angry, they lose their minds and use their kids as pawns in a sick and twisted game. Add in the lure of addictive substances and behavior that boys seek...to numb their minds, such as sex, alcohol, drugs, pornography, or myriad other activities and substances that will provide a good old-fashioned adrenaline rush.

Take away family stability, meaningful spiritual guidance in churches, healthy eating practices, patriotic stories, and extended family. Add a huge dose of violent video games, junk food, rage, neglect, and free time.

Stir it all into our litigious society where we see violent young men coddled and protected while they treat normal boys as aggressive predators for doing normal boy stuff. And we are shocked to find that we have a volatile situation brewing in our culture?

Permission to be Tough
Raising Boys to be Rugged Gentlemen
Tim Austin

Sprinkle on a dash of rudeness, bullying, browbeating, intimidation, and disrespect. Let it simmer in a hormone-crazed environment with cleavage, short shorts, belly button rings, and see-through tops—and what you have is a powder keg of raw emotion... just waiting to explode in our schools, malls or anywhere kids gather.

And we are shocked to find that we have a volatile situation brewing in our culture?

Permission to be Tough
Raising Boys to be Rugged Gentlemen
Tim Austin

SECTION II

TIME TO ENGAGE

***

A gentleman is one who puts more into the world than he takes out.

~ George Bernard Shaw (1856-1950)
Irish playwright, critic, polemicist, and political activist.

***

Permission to be Tough
Raising Boys to be Rugged Gentlemen
Tim Austin

CHAPTER 15
ACTIVITIES TO RAISE RUGGED
GENTLEMEN

*The greatness of a man is not in how much wealth
he acquires, but in his integrity and his ability to
affect those around him positively.*

~ Bob Marley (1945-1981)
Musician

THIS IS WHERE the rubber meets the road. Up to now most of the discussion has centered on theory and philosophy. Following are several suggested activities to do with your son and his friends to guide and push them toward becoming Rugged Gentlemen. Many of these activities were specifically designed to do with a group of a dozen to two dads and boys. Activities with a group are much more fun and the boys gain the benefit of shoulder to shoulder companionship.

Activities for adolescent and high school age boys are actually fun and easy for the most part. I would caution dads to avoid getting all twisted up in complicated, extended,

Permission to be Tough
Raising Boys to be Rugged Gentlemen
Tim Austin

expensive activities. If you know how to shoot a gun and do it safely, it is a cinch to buy a $4 box of clay targets to set out against a dead tree and $4 worth of .22 shells to entertain a group of boys for a whole afternoon. By the way, shooting clay targets or spinner targets are much more fun than shooting paper targets. With clay targets you actually destroy something. With spinner targets exciting stuff happens if you hit your mark.

The activities that are listed are simply ideas to get you started thinking. Feel free to come up with an entirely different set of activities for your son. Most of the activities are fairly inexpensive, extremely easy to plan, are not time-consuming, and are not complicated. Most of these activities require little gear or equipment but are as much fun as they are a learning activity. In fact, if you don't tell the boys it is a learning activity, they will never know it. The toughest part about the whole thing may be finding a place to camp or stay for many of the activities. A farm or ranch might be the ticket for those of you who aren't lucky enough to live in a state where 50% of the land is National Forest. So, you will notice that the activities listed are skewed toward Colorado outdoor adventures. Since most people in this world don't live in Colorado, you will have to select activities for your area.

As you will see the activities listed help a boy grow—body, mind, heart, and soul. They give boys a wide variety of skill, knowledge and understanding. I encourage you to choose a variety of activities that are wild, sedate, crazy, meticulous, hard, easy, tough, soft, powerful, mundane, weak, strong, courageous, and comfortable. Ultimately, the

Permission to be Tough
Raising Boys to be Rugged Gentlemen
Tim Austin

goal is to lend boys courage, humility, and wisdom as they participate. If a boy learns little of the actual skill for each activity but gains courage to try new things, humility to learn new things and wisdom for the future, the time spent will be priceless. Most of us men tend to view the activity as the ultimate goal. In reality, the ultimate goal is to raise a fine young man. When you keep the real goal in mind, it is much easier to plan activities and make decisions that are more beneficial to the boys.

One thing about planning activities for boys is the need for unstructured downtime. While some boys lead sedentary lifestyles and need lots of activity, others are remarkably busy with school, sports, homework, weekend activities and friends. Some boys need that downtime. Planning activities loosely is a good idea in some cases. Boys can entertain themselves for hours with a stick and a mud puddle. And there is nothing wrong with letting them do just that. One of the favorite activities of all the groups I have led was to teach the boys to build a campfire and watch them entertain themselves for hours. Don't feel like you have to jam several activities into each outing.

Before tackling an activity, determine the appropriate level of skill and expertise needed to approach it. For example, a dad who builds houses might involve his son with building an entire home while a dad who is a doctor might be in a bit over his head attempting to build a backyard shed with his son. On the other hand, the doctor might take pleasure in field dressing a deer with his son and showing and teaching about the major components of anatomy. All the while the builder field dressing a deer with his son

117

Permission to be Tough
Raising Boys to be Rugged Gentlemen
Tim Austin

figures "parts is parts, get rid of the guts and let's get this thing to the freezer." Some activities, probably most, need to be approached casually and laid back with flexibility and patience. A few activities need to be approached with vigor, research, planning, aggression, and seriousness.

The activities listed are best attempted with dads and boys together when possible. I encourage dads to invite other boys whose dads may have never experienced anything rugged. It is a good chance to expand the world of a dad and his son at the same time. After many of the activities that my sons and I planned with other boys and dads, many dads expressed their gratitude for getting to do something they missed out on as a boy. And frankly, you, the leader of the band may have to demonstrate your own sense of adventure and courage in planning activities you have never personally participated in yourself. And if you have the guts to give it a go, my hat is off to you. Not only that but if you try something and "fail", you have my double respect. Because that means you stretched out and tried something beyond your capability. That means you had the guts to reach for something big. Just don't get in over your head in a life-threatening way. But know that some bruises, scrapes and maybe even a broken bone or two are okay. Just don't let anyone get permanently maimed or killed.

The activities are varied so that different dads with expertise in different activities can casually and skillfully lead activities. There is nothing like having a few really competent dads along helping the boys and leading activities when assigned. One word of caution; don't invite a know-it-all dad or a dad who has something to prove. It looks bad

Permission to be Tough
Raising Boys to be Rugged Gentlemen
Tim Austin

when one dad has to face-down another dad in front of his son for doing something dangerously stupid or out of line. And when it comes to activities like weapons training, never invite anyone along, boy or adult, that you have any doubt about them listening and following instructions of the "range master". Likewise, on mountain climbs everyone must follow and obey the "climbing guide", or if hunting everyone must follow the "hunting guide".

Helping other men and dads to develop their Rugged Gentleman qualities, along with their son, is a worthwhile goal. The Rugged Gentleman knows when to lead and when to follow. Dads can model both behaviors while doing these activities.

I strongly encourage you to consider asking boys to join you who don't have a dad around. The activities are intentionally planned to be very laid back, informal, and easy yet profound to the boys. The caution is that some of the activities are truly dangerous, those handling weapons and mountain climbing, specifically. Be careful that parents know this, are okay with it, understand the safety expectations and will not bring legal action against you for emotional trauma to their little cupcake if he sees someone shoot a rabbit to fry.

The most profound word of advice I can offer is to simply use wisdom when deciding, planning, and implementing activities. Just use your common sense. For instance, if weather moves in when attempting to climb a 14er, turn around and get everyone off the mountain or to a lower elevation as quickly as it can safely be done. There is a thin line between bravery and stupidity sometimes.

Permission to be Tough
Raising Boys to be Rugged Gentlemen
Tim Austin

Modeling courage and bravery is sometimes the appropriate thing, but sometimes exercising wisdom and caution are far more appropriate.

Don't let my comments scare you, go for it. Have fun. And don't worry about doing stuff perfectly. You will make mistakes, especially when doing activities you have never done before.

WINTER SURVIVAL

FOR THOSE OF you who live in snow country, an afternoon on snowshoes or cross-country skis can give you a wealth of experience. Building a snow cave is quite simple and is great fun for the boys.

LOCATION:

Find a place at higher elevation where the snow accumulates several feet deep.

An unmaintained mountain pass, drill road or mining claim road is perfect.

Find a deep drift where the boys can dig into a vertical face if possible.

ACTIVITY:

Dig out a space sufficient for a couple of boys and their gear.

Use snowshoes, skis, or shovels if you have them.

Pile snow to block the wind at the entrance of the snow caves.

Make sure they don't seal themselves in an airtight space for long periods of time.

Permission to be Tough
Raising Boys to be Rugged Gentlemen
Tim Austin

Build a fire out in the open and boil water for hot chocolate.

Show them how to get a good smoky fire built for a signal for help.

It may take an hour or two to heat up water.

LESSONS TO LEARN:

Discuss when it is best to hole up and when is it best to head down for help.

Discuss hiding or surviving long term in those conditions.

Talk about the proper gear and the consequences of lousy equipment.

Point out the skill and wisdom that is required to survive in harsh conditions.

MOUNTAIN CLIMBING (NON-TECHNICAL CLIMB)

For those of you lucky enough to live in or visit any of our great mountain states, you will have an opportunity that will test your physical and mental ability. Climb one of our nation's tallest mountains. Use common sense and remember that even experienced climbers turn around when threatened by weather, adverse conditions, or fatigue.

LOCATION:

Choose wisely the mountain and route

Some climbs are an easy morning walk and others are grueling two-day adventure.

Permission to be Tough
Raising Boys to be Rugged Gentlemen
Tim Austin

Stay off of technical climbs until you are well seasoned in the sport.

Choose a route most of the boys can hack.

ACTIVITY:

Wear good footwear and layers of clothing.

Leave early enough in the morning that you can get to the summit before noon.

Get off the summit the minute you see the weather building or lightning.

Climb as a group, stronger helping the weaker.

Everyone carries his own day pack with food, water, and survival gear: matches, foil blanket, knife, dry socks, jacket, moleskin, sunscreen, and hat.

Let slow climbers hang on to strong climbers to speed up the ascent.

Absolutely nobody is left behind on the ascent or descent.

Everybody makes it, or nobody makes it.

Be sure you stay hydrated and keep sunscreen applied.

LESSONS TO LEARN:

Teamwork is the way everyone gets to the top.

Some big tough kid may sit down and cry while wimpy little guys pull the bigger boy's whiney butt to the top.

Permission to be Tough
Raising Boys to be Rugged Gentlemen
Tim Austin

Be **mentally prepared** as the adult

When you get exhausted you may have to play games in your own mind to keep going.

When tired take 10 steps at a time and then, rest.

Speed is not the goal

Straighten each leg every single step. It's an old country boy trick.

Encourage, cajole, coerce, or coach exhausted kids to keep moving.

Schedule a trip to a local hot springs pool at the end of the climbing day.

Help boys recognize their need to be physically strong and tough.

SHOOTING

BE SURE TO find a safe place to teach boys to shoot against a dirt berm or dead log. This is one activity that must be closely supervised.

LOCATION:

Find a safe place to shoot

Heck come to Colorado and go out on National Forest land and shoot.

Be safe

ACTIVITY:

Always start kids on single shot .22 rifles or another small-bore weapon.

Permission to be Tough
Raising Boys to be Rugged Gentlemen
Tim Austin

Let them work out their fears on an easy weapon to operate.

Hearing protection is a must and eye protection are appropriate in most situations.

Set clay targets, spinner targets, paper targets or other appropriate knick-knack targets at a sensible distance.

Let the boys get accustomed to shooting longer distances as their skill improves.

As boys mature and grow and develop the bone and muscular structure to handle high-powered rifles, move them up.

As they develop the bone and muscle structure as well as hand-eye coordination to handle shotguns and thrown clay targets, move them up.

As they develop maturity and safety skills, only then would you want to move them into handguns.

Personally, after high-school age is probably most appropriate for most boys to learn to handle handguns.

Handguns are only for a very mature, sensible young man.

Take your time moving boys into weapons that are appropriate. Several trips to the range with one weapon may be the most appropriate.

I highly recommend professional weapons training for young men learning how to protect himself and his family with a weapon.

Permission to be Tough
Raising Boys to be Rugged Gentlemen
Tim Austin

If you do this prior to purchasing a handgun, you will make a smarter purchase of a weapon more appropriate for the shooter.

Always observe sensible range rules

The designated "range master" briefs all participants, instructs target placement, range safety, firing line integrity, reload, misfire, and muzzle safety rules.

I recommend that one safety infraction disqualifies a boy from continuing to participate until the next day.

Sitting in the truck watching others shoot may be adequate reminder to never point a muzzle at another person, for any reason.

Take your time on the range

Clean up your shooting area

LESSONS TO LEARN:

Trustworthiness with a powerful tool

Teamwork

Firearm safety is a must

Talk with boys about defending his family.

Talk with them about never brandishing a weapon.

Teach the importance of respect but not fear of a weapon.

Teach them the importance of being a protector of society.

Permission to be Tough
Raising Boys to be Rugged Gentlemen
Tim Austin

Demonstrate and teach that a weapon is a powerful tool that can be used to destroy, protect. or to provide food.

Help boys recognize the awesome power and responsibility that a weapon in their hands represents.

Never show off with weapons in front of kids. If you own an automatic sport rifle, fine, leave it at home.

Weapons are not toys; they are immensely powerful tools.

Weapons are nothing to fear, but they should always be respected.

Hunter Safety Certification

MOST STATES OFFER a certification course for beginning hunters to ensure that all safety and legal requirements are understood. Most courses are fairly easy and informative. They are sometimes taught by State Wildlife officers. Caution: try to find one taught by experienced weapons experts and experienced hunters who aren't trying to show off and prove how much they know with braggadocios stories and examples. Kids need to learn in a healthy, fact-based, and no-nonsense environment.

ACTIVITY:

Find a course and enroll your kids.

Daughters should take the course also

Anything that gets them familiar with and over any fear of guns is a good thing.

Permission to be Tough
Raising Boys to be Rugged Gentlemen
Tim Austin

Respect for guns is vital, fear can be debilitating.

Attend the class and help your young man learn as much as possible.

LESSONS TO LEARN:

Gun safety

Hunting regulations

Ethical treatment of animals

Respect for the environment

To waste meat is disrespectful to the animal that gave its life so you could live.

Help boys recognize the significance of being able to provide for their families.

COTILLION CLASS

GOOD BEHAVIOR AND good manners have never gone out of vogue in the upper class of society. Only people who have no self-respect, are depraved in their minds, have a chip on their shoulder, feel a need to prove their worth, or feel the need to threaten and bully other people abandon good manners.

In many cities you can find a cotillion, etiquette, dance, manners or social graces class for boys and girls. These classes can be one class or several in a series. These classes give boys a sense of pride and courage to handle social situations of all kinds. Boys need to learn table manners, social graces, dance, manners with adults, manners with

Permission to be Tough
Raising Boys to be Rugged Gentlemen
Tim Austin

girls, and basic social etiquette. A tentative lad will gain immense self-confidence and courage in a well-run class.

ACTIVITY:

Find and enroll your kids in a cotillion or etiquette class.

Find training in a setting where failure is expected along with growth and improvement.

LESSONS TO LEARN:

Good manners and social aptitude help a boy's self-esteem and self-image.

Courage and mental toughness

Exquisite behavior

Eliminate fumbling clumsiness and embarrassment in elegant settings.

Learn and grow into well-mannered individuals.

When boys must ask girls to dance and girls must dance if asked, the pressure is off.

COOK AND CLEAN

BOYS HAVE NO clue what is required to prepare and clean up after a meal. This activity gives him a good chance to understand what mom or dad go through to feed the family. This activity can be done anytime with mom or dad.

ACTIVITY:

Plan a menu

Accompany mom or dad to the grocery.

Cook the meal

Permission to be Tough
Raising Boys to be Rugged Gentlemen
Tim Austin

Serve the family

Clean up afterward

Let your son buy everything for the meal with his own money.

Grilling and outdoor cooking

Lighting the grill

Brushing the rack

Preparing the meat

LESSONS TO LEARN:

- Meal planning
- Budgeting
- Buying the food
- Cooking
- Set the table service
- Clean up
- He will learn to serve his family.
- Moms and dads will learn more than their son as they sit and bite their lip watching the boy goof up.

AUTOMOBILE MAINTENANCE

BOYS OFTEN HAVE a natural curiosity about automobiles. Give them a chance to get dirty and learn about basic car maintenance. Even in the early teen years, this skill can come in handy in case mom has a flat tire or needs to have her

Permission to be Tough
Raising Boys to be Rugged Gentlemen
Tim Austin

vehicle serviced. This activity is best done all at once, so the boy understands what each part of the car is designed to do.

ACTIVITY:

Change the oil and filter

Check all fluids and top off each type of fluid.

Change a tire by locating the jack, safely using the jack to lift the car, locating the spare tire, and putting it on and then taking it back off and stowing it properly.

Check brake pads

Check wiper blades

Check bulbs

Check fuses

Check belts and hoses

Change air filter

Change fuel filter

LESSONS TO LEARN:

Serving the family by helping to maintain the vehicles.

Understanding his place as a protector and helper.

Understanding of the masculine world of the auto parts store.

Understanding how to maintain his own vehicle in a few short years.

Fill the tank with gas for mom every time dad is not around.

Permission to be Tough
Raising Boys to be Rugged Gentlemen
Tim Austin

Check the fluids

Change a flat tire for mom if she ever has a flat.

Vehicle maintenance can save time and money.

Knowledge to diagnose problems and prevent being jerked around by mechanics.

LAUNDRY AND HOUSE CLEANING

Many boys have no clue what happens between the time they throw a dirty shirt into the clothes hamper and it shows up neatly folded on their bed. It will give him a means of understanding how daily chores and daily function of the household works. This activity gives him a good idea of what moms or dads do to keep the family in clean clothes and the house in order.

ACTIVITY:

Separate the clothes by color and fabric.

Load the washer

Add detergent

Set the proper cycle

Separate clothes

Load the dryer

Fold clothes

Put clothes away in their proper place.

If you do your laundry at a Laundromat, this lesson is taught similarly.

Operate a vacuum cleaner

Permission to be Tough
Raising Boys to be Rugged Gentlemen
Tim Austin

Wash windows

Change light bulbs

Conduct home repairs

Wash dishes

Drywall repair

Painting

Door repair

Plunge toilet

Disassemble trap under sinks and reassemble

LESSONS TO LEARN:

Service to the family

Avoid messing up more clothes than necessary.

Wear clothes more than once before laundering.

Keep the house in order

Take care of himself and his needs.

SELF DEFENSE / MARTIAL ARTS / WRESTLING

Sometime in your son's life he may be faced with a situation where he has to physically defend himself or someone else in an altercation. Having the physical ability, skill, and confidence to do so is paramount. The reality is that if a man has the physical ability to defend himself and others, it is likely he won't have to. Bullies, cowards, wife beaters and arrogant jerks know when they are in for a real battle and will usually back down.

Permission to be Tough
Raising Boys to be Rugged Gentlemen
Tim Austin

ACTIVITY:

Sign your son up with a good dojo or wrestling program.

Sign your son up for football

Good coaches push the boys and set tough but reasonable expectations...generally higher than a mom thinks is reasonable.

Let the coach or sensei do his job, to teach, discipline, help, encourage, and push.

Don't interfere with a coach (unless he is doing something blatantly dangerous or disrespectful).

Most boys are capable of 100 times more than they produce on their own.

LESSONS TO LEARN:

Confidence

Mental toughness

Self-discipline

Strategic thinking skills

Patience and tenacity

Having a Rugged Gentleman believe in your son, push him to achieve and give him the skills and experience to do a good job is profound in the life of a boy.

Personal responsibility

Physical toughness

Permission to be Tough
Raising Boys to be Rugged Gentlemen
Tim Austin

Protector of others

Lose gracefully

Win honorably

Sportsmanship and fair play

Good attitude

Compete honorably

Consistent, focused effort

Performing with excellence

These sports teach much more than winning and losing.

DESIGN AND BUILD A STRUCTURE

If you need a garage, tree house, barn, or storage shed, this is your chance to build one with your son. This activity teaches boys the importance of being able to plan, design, purchase materials, and build a useful structure. It can be done from a kit if you don't have the skills to build it from bulk lumber. You may want to involve a builder or framer to help so that the kids learn the proper way to build. Research and obey all local building codes. We don't want to teach the kids how to be renegades, no matter how ridiculous the local codes may be.

ACTIVITY:

Determine what structure is needed

Determine the materials to be used

Determine the basic design

Permission to be Tough
Raising Boys to be Rugged Gentlemen
Tim Austin

Draft the plans, show floor plan, side views and end views.

Solicit help at the lumber yard if you need it.

Draw up a materials list. The guys at the lumber yard will be glad to help you.

Buy more than you need, waste is a normal part of construction.

If it is small enough, design the building on skids to making it portable.

This usually allows you to build outside the building codes.

Check with the local authorities

Have a great time building your structure together.

LESSON TO LEARN:

Proper planning

Structural design

Proper and safe use of construction tools.

Proper ways to deal with the authority of the local building department.

Getting accustomed to the masculine world of the lumber yard.

ATTEND A COLLEGE OR PROFESSIONAL SPORTS EVENT

The world of sports is still full of masculine men. Weak and effeminate men seldom rise to the top in sports. At the same time, it is possible to see disrespect, bad attitudes, cheating, and rudeness in sports.

Permission to be Tough
Raising Boys to be Rugged Gentlemen
Tim Austin

ACTIVITY:

Attend a professional baseball, football, or hockey game.

Attend a college wrestling tournament or martial arts event.

Introduce your son to a world-class athlete if possible.

LESSONS TO LEARN:

Discuss sportsmanship with your boy

Point out how tough, courageous, skilled, and masculine the men are.

Give your son permission to be tough, courageous, skilled, and masculine.

Inspire him to develop great character, patience, faith, and tenacity.

Discuss mental toughness with your boy

Discuss arrogance and humility with him

FISHING

Many men who grew up fishing relish the opportunity to get away from the world by visiting their favorite fishing hole. Fishing is one of the best activities for men to invite boys to participate.

ACTIVITY:

Get the proper license and know the possession limit of fish.

Permission to be Tough
Raising Boys to be Rugged Gentlemen
Tim Austin

Hire a fishing guide if you don't know what you are doing.

Take your son stream fishing

Take him boating

Take your son fly fishing

Proper gear is a must

Go fishing with someone who knows what he is doing.

Relax and enjoy the time together

Teach your boy how to dress and clean the fish.

LESSON TO LEARN:

Patience is a must

Humility is nearly always a part of fishing.

Attracting fish and understanding their habits is important.

Learning to deal with equipment failure is a must.

Helping a boy to do his part in feeding the family is important for him to learn.

Demonstrate your faith in a boy's abilities by letting him fish.

SKIING / SNOWMOBILING

If you happen to live in snow country, some of the best masculine activities can be found out on the snow. These activities typically require a good deal of financial commitment to pull them off, however. Both skiing and snowmobiling are best done with a group of guys.

Permission to be Tough
Raising Boys to be Rugged Gentlemen
Tim Austin

ACTIVITY:

Take your sons skiing or snowmobiling

Enjoy the beauty of the creation

See who can jump the furthest just to make it more interesting.

No screaming like a banshee when you hit jumps. It makes you sound like a beginner.

Obey common sense safety rules

LESSONS TO LEARN:

The need for adrenaline can be met in ways that don't endanger your life, much.

Gravity and horsepower are both fun to work with, not against.

If your old man is made of money; feel free to help him spend your inheritance.

Proper equipment makes winter outings a lot more fun.

PASSPORT TO PURITY

An organization called Family Life puts out an incredible series on sexuality and respect for those of the opposite sex. It is an easy way to teach adolescents the whole birds and the bees lesson by simply loading your CD player and letting it do the heavy lifting. And if you think using the term "heavy lifting" is inappropriate when it comes to talking with your kids about sex, wait until you have to share this bit of

Permission to be Tough
Raising Boys to be Rugged Gentlemen
Tim Austin

knowledge with your kids. It can be a real chore, or it can be amazingly easy if you let Family Life do it. You decide.

I highly recommend listening to the program with your child. Asking questions and engaging in conversation with your child is always a good thing. This activity is best completed when a boy is 10 – 12 years old. This is a great opportunity for a parent to demonstrate open communication and honest dialog with their child, so that the lines of communication will be open forever. It is always a good thing to openly discuss important life issues and respectfully persuade kids to follow the path of humility, service, righteousness, truth, patience, and kindness in their lives.

ACTIVITY:

Order workbooks and CDs through Family Life.

Plan a whole day away in the mountains or on a lake somewhere.

Invite several boys and their dads to participate, it is less embarrassing for the boys.

Start early and play the CDs between fun activities such as swimming, hiking, fishing, or shooting.

LESSONS TO LEARN:

Boys will learn the basics of human sexuality.

Respect for girls and women

Basic roles of men in our society.

Responsibilities of men in a healthy family.

139

Permission to be Tough
Raising Boys to be Rugged Gentlemen
Tim Austin

Camaraderie is a good thing when an embarrassing subject is being discussed.

Respect for our Creator

CPR AND FIRST AID

Learning to be a Rugged Gentleman is about gaining skill in protecting and serving your fellow man. This includes in times of emergencies and trauma.

ACTIVITY:

Enroll your son in a First Aid / CPR class.

Push him to learn and be prepared to aid in an emergency. The life he saves could be yours.

Discuss with him the necessary response to different emergencies involving trauma.

Help him to learn survival skills in any kind of situation.

Teach him common sense ways to apply his knowledge.

Teach him to react calmly and appropriately in a tense situation.

Teach him to protect himself with reasonable precautions.

LESSONS TO LEARN:

Cool-headed action is always better than panic and hysteria.

Permission to be Tough
Raising Boys to be Rugged Gentlemen
Tim Austin

With responsible citizenship comes being prepared to help others in any kind of emergency.

Humanity needs strong men willing to manage the turmoil of an emergency.

There is nothing like preparation when an emergency does occur.

There is a time to roll up your sleeves and there is a time to call for help.

WEEKEND ON THE FARM

As our society gets further and further removed from the farm, we have no appreciation or understanding of where our food comes from. Farm families are hardworking people who are generally respectful of the land, respectful of other people and respectful of their Creator.

ACTIVITY:

Find a farm family who is willing to put up with a bunch of city boys.

Plan a weekend of work on a farm.

Let the boys see how food is produced.

Let them experience what real work actually is.

Encourage the boys to talk with the farmer and understand a different worldview.

Help the boys to understand the principle of sowing and reaping.

Permission to be Tough
Raising Boys to be Rugged Gentlemen
Tim Austin

LESSONS TO LEARN:

Farming is a business of patience

Trust in our Creator and the natural order of the world is an important lesson for a boy to learn.

It never hurts to learn hard work. Cut up hands and a blister here and there are good for a boy to experience.

The principle of sowing and reaping is important in many more facets of life than farming.

In times when men were one crop away from starvation, planting a seed takes faith that it will grow and produce enough food for the year.

Our Creator set up the world to work a certain way. Fight it and mother nature wins. Work with it and you win.

The miracle of life is found in a dead seed.

An apple may have only 4 seeds that could contain a million bushels of apples.

VOLUNTEER

The value of volunteer work is incalculable. There are a myriad of people working in organizations trying to help people who desperately need help. Volunteering will give boys a new perspective on life they may have never seen.

ACTIVITY:

Call the organizers of the local soup kitchen or Red Cross shelter.

Permission to be Tough
Raising Boys to be Rugged Gentlemen
Tim Austin

Call the Salvation Army or a nursing home.

Visit a hospital with toys for hurting children.

Spend a day with your son helping someone who needs a helping hand.

Clean up junk from property nobody maintains.

Shovel the snow from someone's driveway

Write personal notes of encouragement

Practice acts of kindness and goodness for people around you.

LESSONS TO LEARN:

It's not about you

Your time, effort and energy are priceless when you invest them in others.

Other people need you

People are the most valuable thing in the creation.

Words are powerful

CAMPING

The best way to teach a boy is in his element. Camping allows for fire, water, smoke, dirt, animals, and possibly weapons. You can't compile a list that would come nearer to heaven, for a boy.

ACTIVITY:

Plan a camping trip

Plan the food menu

Permission to be Tough
Raising Boys to be Rugged Gentlemen
Tim Austin

Choose a place with water if possible.

Teach your son to pack his own backpack, pitch a tent, and effectively use camp equipment.

Let him gather firewood and build a fire.

Teach him to fish, dress a fish and cook a fish over the fire.

Let him play in the water, mud, or other handy playground materials.

Teach him responsible use and care of the environment.

Let him see your respect for the resources of the earth by the way you deal with nature.

If in season, let him shoot a rabbit or squirrel, dress it, and cook it.

Clean up before leaving

Leave it like you found it

Pick up trash along the way

LESSONS TO LEARN:

Dirt doesn't hurt much of anything

Ruggedness is a masculine trait that is particularly good.

Fire is good in its place, but bad if not respected.

Don't waste

Respect our earth and use resources wisely.

Permission to be Tough
Raising Boys to be Rugged Gentlemen
Tim Austin

READ ABOUT RUGGED GENTLEMAN

There are many great books available on raising boys to be respectful, honorable, courageous, and full of character. I suggest reading some of those books and writing down half a dozen or so of the most important aspects of a first-rate man as you see it. These would be the most important from your perspective. Your son needs to understand your heart, mind, and soul. He needs to see a model of the Rugged Gentleman. You are his hero. He will listen to you.

ACTIVITY:

Read books such as *Wild at Heart* – Eldredge, *Raising a Modern-Day Knight* – Lewis, *Five Aspects of Man* – Mouser, *Raising Boys* – Dobson, or *Boys!* – Beausay II.

Review this list – hard worker, leader, protector, provider, wise chooser, follower of the Creator, teacher, seeker of excellence, compassionate, powerful, full of character, full of integrity, self-disciplined, servant, courageous, loyal, humble, tough, gentle, kind, warrior, rugged, and gentleman.

Choose the words that best encompass your vision and direction for your son.

Write out the list and have it printed on a background that is worthy of framing and hanging on the wall.

Review the vision you have for your son.

Permission to be Tough
Raising Boys to be Rugged Gentlemen
Tim Austin

LESSONS TO LEARN:

Boys need someone to validate, affirm and coach them through life.

Dads are often the most important person in the life of a boy.

Giving a boy a vision is akin to giving him a monument on a distant hill to keep his eyes on and give him a straight path to a distant goal.

Boys are lost and may wander aimlessly the rest of their lives if they do not receive a vision for life or understand their purpose for their existence on earth.

Words are powerful – they build or destroy.

The role of his Dad is profound and paramount in the life of a boy.

FAMILY BUDGET

To be responsible young men, boys must learn to handle family financial matters in a mature way. The alternative is to let him get out on his own and figure out financial issues after he has racked up thousands of dollars of debt, has been led astray by evil friends or develops slothful habits that ruin him financially. Responsible money management is not practiced automatically, it is learned.

ACTIVITY:

Draft a family budget using historical data from past years.

Permission to be Tough
Raising Boys to be Rugged Gentlemen
Tim Austin

Review the budget with your son

Let him sit and watch you pay bills for the month.

Explain to him the fixed costs of running the household such as utility costs, insurance costs, debt payments, and tuition costs.

Explain to him the variable costs of running a household such as home maintenance, phone bill, auto maintenance, speeding tickets, or medical expenses.

Explain discretionary expenditures such as the cost of eating out, tickets to the movie, vacation expenses, or continuing education expenses.

Help him to understand margin and the idea of saving for rainy days.

Help him to understand charitable giving and time investments in other people.

Encourage him to save 10% of everything he makes for retirement, save 10% of what he makes for rainy days and unforeseen emergencies, and give 10% of what he earns to generously help his fellow man. (Richest Man in Babylon)

Encourage him to invest in himself with education, skills, experience, classes, memberships, and organizations.

Encourage him to invest in other people to serve them well and improve their plight in life.

Encourage him to live within his means.

Permission to be Tough
Raising Boys to be Rugged Gentlemen
Tim Austin

LESSONS TO LEARN:

Live responsibly financially

Live a life of generosity

Manage the slavery of debt very carefully.

Improve yourself at every opportunity

Live within your means

Live life with margin so that one mishap doesn't ruin you financially.

HORSEPOWER AND SPEED

Boys need to see what grown men can do with horsepower and speed. Some men never "grow up" by everyone else's definition. The truth is that if you can teach your son to find a job he loves; he will never have to "work" a day in his life.

POSSIBLE ACTIVITIES:

Take your son to a NASCAR race.

Try NHRA drag racing if you want incredible speed and power.

Tractor pulls are incredible displays of raw power and horsepower.

Speed boat races are awe-inspiring events.

Local small oval or dirt track racing can be a hoot.

Sprint bikes and drag bikes are incredibly powerful small engines.

Permission to be Tough
Raising Boys to be Rugged Gentlemen
Tim Austin

Moto-cross and Snow-cross are a ton of fun to watch incredible skill and speed.

LESSONS TO LEARN:

Life is not all about responsibility and work.

Horsepower and speed are fun

Adrenaline rush is good if it is under control.

Safety is the reason fun can happen repeatedly.

Courage comes in many forms

FORMAL DANCE

Formal occasions can be very intimidating to a boy, but boys must learn to handle situations when they are full of fear. A formal function is a non-fatal way for a boy to learn to overcome fear and intimidation.

ACTIVITY:

Take your son with you if you ever have to attend a formal gathering.

Teach him about appropriate attire and image.

Teach him dance and etiquette (Cotillion)

Teach him table etiquette (Cotillion)

Push him to participate, relax and have fun.

LESSON TO LEARN:

Formal behavior and etiquette

Permission to be Tough
Raising Boys to be Rugged Gentlemen
Tim Austin

Image and attire are important in all parts of life.

If you look good and feel good about yourself, it will show in your actions.

Dance is also good to know for later in life.

Boys must learn to be comfortable around females.

Learning good manners at a young age will help tremendously later in life when a man finds himself at informal gatherings.

CHAINSAWS AND PLANTERS

When a boy is fearful, he is tentative and intimidated. But if a man demonstrates trust in him, courage is passed from dad to son. One of the simplest but profound ways to demonstrate your trust in a boy is to let him operate tools, dangerous tools. Chainsaws and axes are some of the most dangerous in the mind of a boy. None of the activities or suggestions in this book are intended to be done with boys who are physically, mentally, or emotionally unprepared or unable to handle the task. Proper use of chainsaws and weapons are only to be taught when boys are ready.

ACTIVITY:

Find a short log, 4'-5' in length by 14" to 24" in diameter, that can be hollowed out for a planter for mom.

With the log laying on the ground, draw a straight line from one end to the other. T*hen draw another line 5" – 7" away parallel to the first.*

Permission to be Tough
Raising Boys to be Rugged Gentlemen
Tim Austin

With a chainsaw, standing over the log, plunge the saw tip into one of the lines. Do not plunge it so deep it cuts out of the bark down below.

Cut two saw kerfs several inches deep at each line but stop about 6" short of the ends of the log.

Take an axe, adze or sharpened pickaxe and dig out all of the wood between the lines.

Gouge the saw tip around the ends and clean the interior of the log. Dress it with the saw.

Drill 3 ¼" weep holes in the bottom of the planter.

Split a 4" diameter piece of firewood in half.

Flip the planter upside down and screw both halves of the split firewood to the bottom for a stable base. Fill it with dirt and plant mom some flowers in it.

LESSONS TO LEARN:

Proper and safe handling of power and hand tools.

Hard work and blisters don't hurt anyone.

Even as adolescents, boys have the ability to produce a cool gift for their moms.

Safety is what allows for fun to be repeated.

Boys have the ability to handle powerful tools.

NURSING HOME

Older members of our society are often laid to rest long before their death. In later stages of life, when they are full of insight, understanding, maturity and wisdom, they are put

151

Permission to be Tough
Raising Boys to be Rugged Gentlemen
Tim Austin

away and largely ignored. None of us want to die alone in a hospital bed that smells like piss in a nursing home that is understaffed by minimum wage earners who don't give a damn about whether or not their job is done at all, let alone done well. The Rugged Gentleman has compassion and love for the older members of his family. Though inconvenient and bothersome at times, he helps his family members live their final years and days in the comfort and care of home. Certainly, there are times when their medical needs are beyond his and his immediate family to handle, but that is an exception. If you want to avoid that same fate when you get old, teaching your children about the priceless value of our older family members is paramount.

ACTIVITY:

Develop a friendship with a person in a nursing home.

Visit them on a regular basis

Talk with older people and develop true relationships.

Care for dying family members at their home if possible.

Take them into your home if needed.

Involve the kids with their care when necessary.

Don't treat death and dying as a mysterious thing to fear, it happens to us all.

Teach your son the importance of developing a deep abiding faith so that death has far less fear and dread.

Permission to be Tough
Raising Boys to be Rugged Gentlemen
Tim Austin

LESSONS TO LEARN:

Life is precious no matter what stage of life a person is in.

Older family members have priceless wisdom and insight that we all need to hear.

Caring for family is not optional, it is necessary.

Expecting the government to care for your older family members is selfish and wrong.

All people have quirks that should be ignored or accepted.

Treat all people with dignity and mercy.

HOME & LANDSCAPE MAINTENANCE

Keeping a home or business place beautiful isn't necessarily automatic. It sometimes takes a great deal of time and effort. Helping a boy to know how to maintain a home and its exterior landscaping is a good idea.

ACTIVITY:

Change light bulbs

Plunge a toilet

Disassemble the trap piping under the sink.

Adjust a door

Apply caulking and weather stripping

Reset a circuit breaker or ground fault circuit interrupter.

Caulk and paint

153

Permission to be Tough
Raising Boys to be Rugged Gentlemen
Tim Austin

Re-stretch carpet

Mow the lawn

Run an edger

Prune trees

Place rock or bark ground cover

Repair a fence

Plant trees, shrubs, or flowers

Trim shrubs

Repair the sprinkler system

Sand and stain a deck

Hang and repair window coverings

Shut off the main water service

Light a pilot light

Build shelves

Assemble furniture

Change out a shower head

Put linens on a bed

Defrost and clean a refrigerator

Build a fire in the fireplace or stove.

Clean a fireplace or stove

Close a damper

Patch a hole in the drywall

Winterize a house

Permission to be Tough
Raising Boys to be Rugged Gentlemen
Tim Austin

LESSONS TO LEARN:

Self-sufficiency

Save money maintaining the house

Appreciation for the Creator's handy work

Respectful stewardship of our earth

EXPLORING

Depending on where you live there are tons of places and things to explore together. Here in Colorado we have more adventures than a dad and son could possibly cover in a lifetime.

ACTIVITIES:

Explore old mines and mining districts

Visit old railroad sites, tunnels, and museums.

Underwater exploring with snorkel or scuba gear.

Explore old historic districts

Visit ancient ruins and ancient cultural sites.

Tour museums, art galleries and exhibits

Mountain bike old railroad beds

Go white water rafting

Explore ghost towns and surrounding areas

LESSONS TO LEARN:

Historic cultural challenges

Hard work and hardy people

155

Permission to be Tough
Raising Boys to be Rugged Gentlemen
Tim Austin

Imagine going back to those times

Appreciate the rugged beauty in the world.

BUILD A COMPUTER

Attempting this miracle for me would be tantamount to climbing Mt. Everest. I struggle with technology and all things technical. So, I feel your pain if you cringe at some of my activities. Both of us need to buck up and go for it.

ACTIVITY:

Plan and design a computer

Purchase components and kits

Assemble computer

Troubleshoot any malfunctions

Start kicking it until it works

LESSONS TO LEARN:

Patience

Tenacity

Computer skills

Electrical component assembly

RAPPELLING / ROCK CLIMBING

One of the greatest fears for most people is falling, especially when there are rock cliffs around. Rappelling is the most wonderful feeling, once you step over the edge. It frees your soul and validates your ability to overcome fear.

Permission to be Tough
Raising Boys to be Rugged Gentlemen
Tim Austin

ACTIVITY:

Take your son rappelling outdoors on natural rock cliffs if possible.

Climbing walls are a good substitute if natural rock is not available.

LESSONS TO LEARN:

Trust

Teamwork

Mental strength

Overcoming fear

PROJECT

Completing a major project with your son can be one of the most satisfying activities you can engage in. This can be anything from something simple and inexpensive to overly complex and costly.

ACTIVITIES:

Soapbox derby car and race

Restore a classic car

Build a shed, garage or house together.

Plan an Alaskan fishing tour

Trek the Andes

Climb Mt. McKinley

Raft the Grand Canyon

Plan a week-long elk hunt

Permission to be Tough
Raising Boys to be Rugged Gentlemen
Tim Austin

Sail the west coast of the U.S.

LESSONS TO LEARN:

Camaraderie

Shared adventure

Appreciate the rugged beauty of the Creation.

Appreciate Rugged Gentlemen along the way.

SPORTS

The world of sports can be the most profound way to teach a boy many of life's lessons. Participating in sports puts a boy in the position of winning and losing, learning to overcome failure, learning to respect the rules, coaches, other players, opponents, and referees. Without respect for the referee an athlete gets tossed from the game. Without respect for his opponent he doesn't take them seriously and gets beat. Without respect for his fellow teammates he openly complains or messes up and the team loses. Without respect for the coach he doesn't pay attention to the strategies and tactics devised to win, therefore assuring the team will lose. Without respect for the rules, your team gets penalized or even disqualified. Sports teach rules in simulated life situations. It is far better to break the rules and be penalized now than to make a life habit of breaking rules to the point you get caught stealing from your employer or selling illegal drugs.

ACTIVITY:

Enroll your son in one sport at a time.

Permission to be Tough
Raising Boys to be Rugged Gentlemen
Tim Austin

Enroll him in various sports

Help him find the sport(s) that help him learn the most, that he enjoys, that fits his physique and skill best, and that he can excel in.

As he gets older, introduce him to sports that he can enjoy all of his life such as golf, racquetball, bowling, or tennis.

Introduce him to sports that you enjoy so that you can find common interests to share once he is grown and out of the house.

Remember your main goal is to grow a healthy young man, not win every game.

Encourage his good attitude, effort, energy, strategic thinking, aggression, fundamentals, and his love for the game.

Validate him with positive words

Let him experience the agony of defeat.

Help him experience the thrill of victory.

Walk with him shoulder to shoulder

Don't preach

Don't care more than your son cares.

Let him be a kid

Avoid telling him how wonderful and perfect he is.

Permission to be Tough
Raising Boys to be Rugged Gentlemen
Tim Austin

LESSONS TO LEARN:

Expose your son to many different activities to help him discover what he is good at and enjoys.

Treat your son with dignity and respect and you will have a friend for life.

Learn to use words to validate, affirm, encourage, accept, acknowledge, and motivate your son.

Use sports as a tool to teach respect.

Raise a young man who is healthy physically, mentally, emotionally, and spiritually.

CHAPTER 16
THE CHALLENGE

*My father didn't tell me how to live; he lived and let
me watch him do it.*

~ Clarence Budington Kellan (1881-1964)
American Writer

ALL MY LIFE I have heard dads complain and moan about
their kids, boys especially. And I think to myself, "what a
shame to see the most important relationship wasted". I
have seen angry young men drain their lives down a rat hole
by ruining their minds with drugs, ruining their body with
laziness, ruining their lives with addictions, and ruining their
families with arrogance. And it breaks my heart to see it.

My goal is to forge a new trail back to some old
traditions and respectful times when men worked side by
side with their precious sons and taught them to be men. I
want to encourage men to recreate those times to some
degree by taking time out from the grind to raise a Rugged

Permission to be Tough
Raising Boys to be Rugged Gentlemen
Tim Austin

Gentleman. The first winners will be the confident, strong young men of character who are built out of the experience. Ultimately, I believe the true winners will be our society as a whole.

As I see fractured families where the old folks go off to die alone and scared, the men are living lives of fear and self-doubt and young people are all twisted up in fear needing someone to blaze a trail and lead them to a better way of living.

This book is but a few steps down that trail of dads and sons walking through life shoulder to shoulder.

When I see a man, whose sons live far away in other states—living, for all intents and purposes, a fatherless life, it sickens me. When I see men living with huge voids in their souls because they didn't receive the validation, encouragement, acceptance, and affirmation from their dads, it breaks my heart.

My aim is to treat my boys with respect. My goal is to live adventures with them. My purpose is to instill in them courage, faith, strength, wisdom, and a humble heart. My intent is to treat them with respect so that I get to be involved in their lives the rest of my life. Ultimately, I hope to be their friend as well as their dad.

In the perspective of a boy, their dad goes from being the big person in their mom's house to the huge hero the boy longs to emulate. Next... dads get to be the boy's protector and teacher, moving them toward independence. During the last years in the home, the dad hopefully becomes the coach and mom the cheerleader as the lad begins to stretch his

Permission to be Tough
Raising Boys to be Rugged Gentlemen
Tim Austin

wings and start learning to fly. At some stage, hence it is my goal to become mentor and friend to my boys. I can't wait to visit that stage of life with them.

May you find the strength to step out in faith, knowing that your boy needs your character and strength to sprout and grow his own.

May the Creator bless you richly as you raise a Rugged Gentleman or become one yourself.

Permission to be Tough
Raising Boys to be Rugged Gentlemen
Tim Austin

ABOUT THE AUTHOR

Tim Austin lives a simple and quiet life on his farm in Paonia, Colorado. He handles business operations and marketing of fruit and fresh produce for his parent's orchard and farm operation. He volunteers as a high school wrestling coach and EMT for the local ambulance service in the off-season. The author loves spending time with grandsons who are his pride and joy. The mountains are his favorite place to be, trail hiking, mountain climbing, bear hunting, elk hunting, stream fishing, backpacking, camping, or just sitting in a grove of aspen trees are but a few activities that add spice and adventure to life.

Tim is a bit of an enigma, loving the extremes of life as much as the *squishy middle*.

He loves risky adventure activities as well as calm and quiet contemplation. While he cherishes solitude, this rugged man can also be the life of the party. He loves the mountains but cherishes time by the ocean; he loves fight sports but relishes the calm and slow pace of sports like golf or baseball. As a writer, he is equally inspired by quiet evenings at home and an exciting night on the town. Austin loves roaring crowds but relishes spending a week on a horse in the mountains without seeing a soul. Tim loves

Permission to be Tough
Raising Boys to be Rugged Gentlemen
Tim Austin

diesel fumes, horsepower and speed but holding his grandson as he sleeps is an incredible delight.

This dedicated father appreciates his family and deep friendships but loves meeting new people. He finds a way to enjoy both the sweltering heat of summer and the frigid cold of winter, softly falling snow or the crash of thunderstorms. He loves adventure, lives life with courage, and hopes others find the same appreciation for life.

Being an "empty-nester" brings new meaning to life for Tim, who thrives on a deep faith and deeper respect for his Creator. While he describes the peace in his soul and patience toward others in ways that are almost beyond understanding... he leans into his love for kids and their sports and continues to volunteer as an EMT and wrestling coach where young boys find a coaching style, which is truly rugged, aggressive, confident, and tough.

Like many of us, Tim's parenting style was a work in progress. Growing up in a legalistic and harsh religion gave him a touch of faith but also many examples of harshness he did not want to repeat with his own kids. While he did his best to give his kids everything they needed, he did not shower them with everything they wanted. Parenting for Tim was learned by fits and starts, failures and triumphs, frustrations and successes, trials and errors, tears, and laughter.

Through it all his kids are incredible human beings. They are compassionate, kind, competent, outgoing, tough, smart, confident, patient, humble, respectful, and courageous. His

Permission to be Tough
Raising Boys to be Rugged Gentlemen
Tim Austin

kids live life with as similar a sense of adventure as their dad raised them with.

The author's first book, *The Exasperated Woman's Guidebook* demonstrates he is not afraid to take on pressing issues that others may not generally talk about. In this book, he hopes to inspire us to look squarely at a current societal issue and consider alternatives. His hope is that this book brings awareness that will motivate us to act and shape the next generation of young men into Rugged Gentlemen who are self-reliant, self-disciplined, thoughtful, kind and gracious yet strong and fierce when the situation calls for it.

Permission to be Tough
Raising Boys to be Rugged Gentlemen
Tim Austin

OTHER BOOKS BY THE AUTHOR

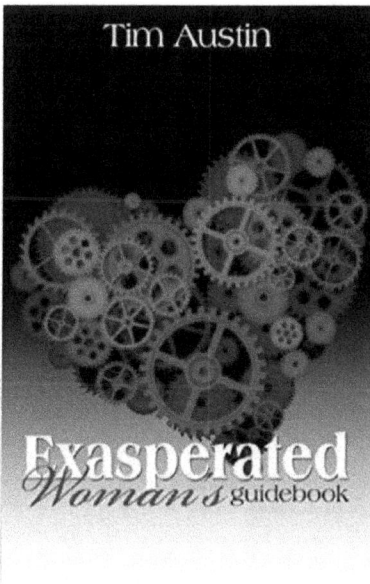

Respectful men live by an unspoken honor code to which women are rarely privy. You can learn to use this unspoken honor code to win his heart, mind, and soul to your side. You don't have to be frustrated, angry and exasperated with your man anymore.

The Exasperated Woman's Guidebook exposes and outs the supposedly secret world that exists between many a man's ears. It is much simpler than you might think.

Paperback: 162 pages
Publisher: Comfort Publishing, LLC; 1 edition (August 1, 2011)
Language: English
ISBN-10: 1936695022 | ISBN-13: 978-1936695027

Permission to be Tough
Raising Boys to be Rugged Gentlemen
Tim Austin

Leave Me a Review!

If you enjoyed this book or found it useful, I would be honored if you would take a moment to leave a review. I'm always interested in learning what you like, think, and want. I read all the reviews personally.

Thank you—in advance—for your support! At the end of the day, it is the reviews and comments made by readers that put the spark in a book—and direct the author about what and how to write in the next one!

You may also want to gift this book to someone whom you feel could benefit from the tools provided here. It is available in print, digital (Kindle), and audio book on Amazon and other popular retailers.

Tim Austin